LIVING A
CONTENTED LIFE

(From Points of Reality)

INYIMA KALU
(Sacred Soldier)

Paperback: 978-1-968667-98-6
Hardcover: 978-1-969919-70-1
eBook: 978-1-968667-99-3
Library of Congress Control Number: 2025921091

This is a work of nonfiction.

Ordering Information:

Prime Seven Media
518 Landmann St.
Tomah City, WI 54660

Printed in the United States of America

CONTENTS

BIBLE VERSIONS AND INITIAL ARRANGEMENT.

{KJV = KING JAMES VERSION} = {NKJV = NEW KING JAMES VERSION} =

{AMP = AMPLIFIED} = {AMPC = AMPLIFIED CLASSIC} =

{NAS = NEW AMERICAN STANDARD} = {ESV = ENGLISH STANDARD VERSION}

DEDICATION

This book, Living a contented life is first dedicated to the almighty God who is contented in every respects from the beginning of his existence which no one knows till now and remains the same forever. Who also created us humans to be like him in every area of life, our living in contentment being the subject matter of this book. But the intrusion of Satan and sin devastate us into compromising. Moreover I dedicate the book to him (God) for restoring my sense, acts and life of contentment by his grace and power of the holy spirit.

The book is also dedicated to all of the people who live in contentment according to God's standard, because I know it's one of the most difficult task anyone can execute. The inability to live a life of contentment is the central reason the majority of the Christians and others never serve God efficiently. Moreso I dedicate the book to all of those who recognise the rich importance of contentment even though they're struggling to live it out, but have the zeal to achieve it. I pray that God helps them to do so in Jesus name.

FOREWARD

All of God laws are laws of contentment and the reason all of us humans had violated any of his laws in the past, and the majority of us are still violating some or all of them, while many have determined to continue to do it till eternity is because of discontentment in our sin polluted nature and character. Only contentment can prepare anybody, positioning him or her very well to be truly humble and receive the baptism of the holy spirit and peculiar grace of God for becoming a God's vessel of honour. Then adding righteousness, knowledge, understanding, wisdom, zeal and consistency result in excellent performance and achievements in the lord God.

Having this revelation, the apostle Paul exhorts that contentment with godliness is great gain. Meaning living a life of contentment in the in the lord is advantageous in all aspects. I pray that God helps me to be consistent with my life of contentment in him and I pray for and encourage all others who are not contented in God to repent and become contented in him, and let all of us work together to live the life of contentment, especially in God, because it lays the foundation for establishing the kingdom of God and his will on earth, which Jesus Christ and his faithful disciples pray for.

PREFACE

The world would be a perfect place to live in if all of us humans have regard for God's law of contentment. Greediness is the fundamental cause of the turmoil all over the places, because almost each individual person wants to have more material possessions, more power of rulership and higher status than others, especially to possess more than his or her rivals in his ventures and ambitions.

Besides war of self superiority caused by ego triggered bogus desires in people, the bogus desires then develops desperation to accomplishing them. This state of the mind makes its victims greedy for powers, social /religious status, wealth, paramount positions of rulership and self glory. Nevertheless: there are people who are not ruled by ungodly desires and desperation, rather they're contented with whatever God provides for them whether materials or intangible honours and potentials. It is true that, greed for self honour and glory have staged our world to become a centre of ungodly competitions and rivalry, yet there are still those who have a proven integrity concerning divine law of contentment, and are therefore not carried away to compete unnecessarily with others. Furthermore; God wills we should be contented with his providence, as we understand that he is able to gratify our needs at all times.

Some people understand what it means to be contented while some do not understand it. Therefore the both of the truly enlightened, the misinformed and the ignorant in most cases assert to be contented, but it can only be proved by discerning from their actions to know who are truly contented and who are not. Personal actions have true revelation of being contented or greedy. Confirmed evidences of contentment manifest in lifestyle as well as evidences of greed do show forth in personal lifestyle.

= MODERATING ACQUISITION =

Barbarity is one of the evidences of greed, which reveal that barbarians are not contented, but are greedy and desperate in possessing more and more even when it has to do with destroying lives and properties of others. But as many as are called the children of the most high God must live their lives in the opposite way to barbarity. That means those who profess godliness must forbid barbarity because it is robbery and violation of God's law of protection.

God forbids the violation of his laws and destruction of lives and properties of others among us humans.

Likewise God's children are obliged to forbid them. Barbarity is just one of the proves of desperation for acquisition, But there are several other ways of being desperate to get rich which may not involve physical assault towards others, yet, The desperate venturers reveal their greediness and desperation for acquiring through the covetousness kinds of businesses, jobs, and much more other activities they execute. So barbarity and all other kinds of covetousness is what the first chapter of the books speaks against, and the chapter also promotes acquiring things by legitimacy.

= MODERATING CONSUMPTION =

Eating, drinking, smoking, inhaling of intoxicating drugs and sex habits are serious issue that, Christians and entire humans are supposed to be well concerned about. Because many at times, Christians like others carelessly eat, drink, smoke / inhale the hard drugs and have sex unethically and thereby abuse what they consume, and themselves who consume them. Ignorance of godly ethics about consumption keeps so many Christians and non Christians in obscure that, excessive and improper ways of eating, drinking, smoking / inhaling of hard drugs, having sex illegally with anybody or anything is a sin. However: there are Christians who are aware of the sin of immodest consumption yet they are unable to overcome it, while there are some other Christians who are aware of it and have overcome it. The cases is the same with the non Christians among whom some are ignorant, some are aware but weak and some aware and overcomers.

It is very common to see most nominal Christians who strive to justify their immoderate alcoholism, inhaling and smoking of intoxicating drugs with the logic that, after all Jesus turned water into wine, some strive to justify their smoking of Marijuana leaves, cigarettes and other intoxicating drug but smokeless with the logic that, all that they smock are made with natural vegetables and other things created by God. But do all the logic the immoderate consumers apply really justify them? Are all of their logics in line with God's principles for consumption?

As I usually say; God's laws and principles are unchangeable, so whatever acts which include consumption manners that contradict God's approved way of consumption are sins. It doesn't matter whom the consumer may be, what really matter is the sure word of God that must be obeyed, and the obedient being for their righteous by consumption or the law to be disobeyed while the disobedient bearing consequences of disobeying God's word starting from here on earth and to eternity if there is no repentance in the process of lives.

Regardless of all that have been said: The principled Christians dare to show forth their righteousness by being careful to accept whatever they eat and drink, and never to inhale or smoke any polluting substance, ensuring they are not carried away to consume abusively.

This is about presenting factual, physical and emotional acts and activities being backed with biblical texts to proven reality of moderate living and venturing by those who exercise reverential fear of God. And also to prove that godly principles as the bible contains are the perfect prerequisites to living out God approved life of discipline and moderation for true contentment in all ramifications of life.

= MODERATING SEXUAL LIFE =

Sex perversion seems to be a normality in this dispensation of life. Those who are sexual puritans are regarded to be uncivilised, because evil is promoted and Righteousness is despised by the majority to the extent that some of the governments legalise sexual perversion and make tax money out of it. A lot of private citizens also make their own money by sexual perversion, and the clients are those who are unable to discipline their sexual appetite. So the third chapter of the book is about the expose of kinds of sexual immoderation and how it causes discontentment, then the principles of sexual moderation and how it brings and develops contentment.

= MODERATING DESIRES =

The fourth chapter of the book is intended to teach on how to recognise the dangers of excess desire of everything and to guide to also recognise the benefits of disciplining ourselves while we desire anything so we should avoid the dangers of greedy desires and to enjoy contentment which is the greatest benefits of moderation and moderate desire being the contextual example on this part.

= MODERATING RELATIONSHIP =

Associating with people can be properly or abused, the way we relate with people matters a lot in our life, because it either contributes to our upliftment or to our downfall. Relationship in marriage, in the church, in the political structure, in businesses, in the educational institutions, in sexual perversion, in robbery, drinking, smoking, eating and so on. There are bad kinds of relationships whether all of us accept the fact to condemn the bad relationships as being disastrous or not. There are also good kinds of relationships whether all of us understand it and justify them or not. It doesn't matter whether someone governments call evil relationships good and call evil relationships good, by legalising the evil relationships and abolishing the good relationships. We are to recognise the both of these conflicting kinds of relationships and to be moderate and contented with our own relationships by avoiding the bad relationships and focus on the good ones and to be with the boundaries of discipline in the good relationships.

= MODERATING ZEAL =

The zeal with caution and the zeal with emotions and self will are two kinds of discrepant seals that builds or destroys. The zeal with caution is the diligent zeal which is constructive to anything in which it's invested, while the zeal with emotions and self will is the rash zeal which is destructive to whatever it is invested into. Most of the troubles people get into and most of the discomfort they get and cause others is just because they're so hasty and unreasonable to engage actions and enact some reckless services, rules and imaginary fulfilments. But when diligent zeal is employed in anything it enables the diligent zealots to be right and certain in their mind before they start anything. And by so doing, they achieve good results and satisfaction to themselves and others.

= MODERATING GIVING =

We are not to be stingy or to be foolishly generous, in the sense that we should not be withholding anything we can comfortably give out to help others and to promote the work of God. And we should not be giving out anything that puts us into pains, frustration and regrets because we are emotional to helping people and to supporting God's work. So our happiness, joy, peace of the mind and emotional satisfaction are at stake in our life of giving, and we are to protect them by being genuine and disciplined in giving.

= MODERATING THOUGHT.

This is about disciplining the mind to be selective with ideas it raises and the ones it receives to keep. There is a regular battle between good and bad ideas in the mind of everyone who is porous to thoughts. A lot of unintentional mistakes and frustration emanating from those mistakes are produced by mixture of good and bad thoughts directing the actions of the porous people. We are to guard or minds therefore to focus in receiving and harbouring only good thoughts so we should not continue to be distracted by bad thoughts and for us to be in control of our minds, actions, results in the positive way beside God who the sovereign master and for living in satisfaction through how good we think and act and the good results they bring.

= MODERATING WORDS =

Careless talking results in committing international and unintentional offenses against humans and sin against God. But diligent talking results in preventing careless offending and sinning. We all know there are personal and external repercussive aftermaths of offenses and sins, and that verbal offenses and sins are unexceptional. We can all attest that no sinner lives a life void of self caused troubles but living a life which does not attract self caused troubles is possible with the righteous. We all are living in the world full of troubles but there are avoidable troubles and unavoidable troubles. Only God can save whoever from the unavailable troubles but we are responsible for saving ourselves from the avoidable troubles and saving our reckless words and using our diligent words is the issue of concern here. Diligence is one of the definitions of moderation, so diligence with words is moderation of words which brings about living in satisfaction through talking prudently.

= CONTROLLING EMOTIONS =

Emotion is inner feeling, emotions are all sorts of inner feelings, how we feel about people, things and situations is a contributing factor to how we act, react or refuse to do anything toward them. Emotions are deceitful and are some of the greatest enemies of humanity, because it makes people to be superficially expressive to circumstances, to people and other things while being driven away from the purposes of doing whatever.

Christianity is a case example of what the majority of humans including the church members practice and react to emotionally: (how they feel about it rather than why they should practice it). Most people act and react to Christianity out of the purpose of it but according to how they feel about it. It makes them to never be satisfied with Christianity and making others to do the same. But those who truly know the purpose of Christianity and deal with it according to purpose grab the benefits which come from it and they live satisfactorily with it. So it is with every other thing of life.

= MODERATING REASONING =

We must eradicate rigid thinking and to adapt to convergent thinking, and besides we are to be positive with the convergent thinking pattern. Rigid thinking whether with good or bad intentions leads to conceitedness. That is the perception of someone to conclude that his or her views and opinions are always the best for everything. But convergent thinking is about comparing personal perceptions to those of others while convergent reasoning is the act of being willing to surrender personal wrong or subordinate views and opinions to right and superior views and opinions of others, or to kindly subdue the wrong and subordinate views and opinions of others with personal right and superior views and opinions. By doing this we are rationally developing reasonable contentment for ourselves and between us and other reasonable people.

= MODERATING LEADERSHIP =

Tyrannical leadership is devastating to the subjects and the devastation rebounds to the tyrants. So nobody ever inherit contentment through wicked leadership, therefore it must be eradicated from any people who chose to experience the contentment of leadership. In this case, leadership should be fair and never unjust because peace, tranquillity and contentment never exist where justice and equity don't exist and leadership is the custody of peace, tranquillity and contentment.

Contentions form the topic of the thirteenth chapter, and contentment through Contention is about never to think that contentions should never arise among people of different segments, but to know how to manage the contentions well, putting the knowledge into action. For overcoming contentions with diligence we are able to live without being preoccupied with them and with the same diligence we are able to prevent most perceived contentions that are yet to arise to keep our life free from worriness of contention progressing.

= BEING TEACHABLE THAN BEING SCORNFUL =

Being teachable is one of the ways to live in peace with self and with the people who teach or correct us, especially when the teaching, the correction and the compliance are genuine. Moderating leaning to have contentment is not about being humble to learning the wrong things from false mentors and correctors but it's about being humble to learning the right things from true mentors and correctors. Every genuine teaching, correction and compliance are part of godliness by education. And everything that is godly provides contentment for the godly people.

= MODERATING DRESSING =

Indecent dressing is offensive and sinful in the sense that grown up girls and ladies who dress seductively put sexual lust into the mind of many boys and men, and the seductive dressing revealing the seductive desire of the women who dress that way. Though a lot of such women are defensively arrogant to claim they don't offend anyone with their erotic dressings but those men who lust after them are the offenders, yet neither them nor the lusters nor my kind that condemn the immoral dressing patterns have peace of mind with it. So the seductive dressing sister should help by changing their dressing modes so to reduce the temptation of sexual lust as much as we able, because I know for certain that even if all of the women in this world begin to dress decently most men will continue to be sexually lustful but we all should cooperate to alleviate lust as much as possible especially in the church. By doing this the people with the fruit of the holy spirit find the platform to be contented with their sexual life.

= MODERATING SPENDING =

This sixteenth and last chapter of the books talks about wise spending as a means of living an economically contented life. There are people who should be rich but they are mediocres or poor regarding wealth, just because they spent the lager amount of their wealth lavishly. There are some other who should be in the middle class of rich but are never stable in that condition because of the same problem of lavish spending. There are poor people who are also lavishly extravagant and are really dissatisfied with their regular financial and resources status. There are also people who are naturally stingy and some of the such spend their resources on the wrong things and are never satisfied, neither satisfying others with it. Whether being rich or poor economic contentment is necessary, and we can attain it by spending moderately and to be satisfied with whatever we legitimately have.

Chapter 1

MODERATING DESIRES.

DEFINITION = MODERATION IS = Doing things properly without extremes and offences.

MEMORY VERSE = *Prov 13:19 ESV = A desire fulfilled is sweet to the soul, but to turn away from evil is an abomination to fools.*

INTRODUCTION

It is in human nature to overdo almost everything pertaining to life and endeavours. The overdoing of things which emanates from lusts, greed, selfishness, pride, untamed ill temper, envy and jealousy, including other manifestations of humans carnality is a stronghold that besets all humans, the Christians, religionists ,socialists and liberals alike. But by the leading of the holy spirit, self discipline, self contentment and the grace of God, the life affairs and desires can be disciplined also. But due to bible illiteracy, obstinacy and reprobation, the divine requirement to live a total moderate life by all, is being ignored, yet, it is humans duty to endeavour to live in God's pleasure through God's required moderation in all aspects of life. As the word of God unveils; that excessiveness and exaggeration of all things is evil, but exhibiting discipline, contentment and total godly humility over humans acts and ventures is righteousness.

Hence all humans should live the life of total discipline and be contented in all that have to do with life and its affairs, because doing thus is one of the ways of us being obedient true children of God. As we know God is a disciplined contented God, who demands that those who truly believe in him should follow suit in his lifestyle so as to be approved children of his.

Desire is the first step to being moderate or immoderate, to being contented or discontented. There is nothing wrong with having desires because it's natural and God takes the lead, but having exaggerated desire is evil because it is the primary evidence of greediness and instigator of covetousness. But being moderate with desires restrict and prevents the desirers from greed and covetousness. The chapters of the book has their various aspects of demands for moderation and of the benefits for it.

---

i = SHUNNING BARBARITY = (Prv 1:10-16) (AMP).

My son, if sinners entice you, do not consent. V 10 . If they say, come with us, let us lie in wait (to shed) blood, let us ambush the innocent without cause(and show that his piety is in vain). V 11 . Let us swallow them alive as does sheol (the place of the dead),and whole, as those who go down into the pit(of the dead. V 12 . We shall find and take all kinds of precious goods(when our victims are put out of the way), we shall fill our house with plunder; V 13 .

Throw in your lot with us (they insist) and be a sworn brother and comrade; let us all have one purse in common. V 14 . My son, do not walk in the way with them; restrain your foot from their path. V 15. For their foot rush to evil, and they make haste to shed blood. V 16 .

= (Prv 4:14-17, AMP) =

Enter not into the path of the wicked, and go not in the way of evil men. V 14 . Avoid it, do not go on it, turn from It and pass on. V 15 For they cannot sleep, unless the have caused trouble or vexation; their sleep is taken away unless they have caused someone to fall. V 16 . For they eat the bread of wickedness and drink wine of violence. V 17.

Two among the major urges which transpire barbarity are greed and desperation to getting rich. But being contented is the best way of countering and conquering the greediness and eagerness to hurting people and acquiring riches and thereby display immoderate attitudes to God and man, which is a clear evidence of infringing the divine law of moderating riches acquiring. So the godly wise are to shun barbarity in their search for riches and dare live satisfactorily with such as God provides for their needs. And to succeed in this requires the discipline over desires.

ii = BEING CONTENTED WITH CURRENT POSSESSIONS = (Prv 13:11, AMP).

Wealth (not earned but)won in haste or unjustly or from the production things for vain or detrimental use(such riches) will dwindle away, but he who gathers little by little will increase (his riches) .

= (Prv 15:16-17, KJV) =

Better Is a little with the reverent, worshipful fear of the Lord than great and rich treasures and trouble there with. V 16 . Better is a dinner of herb where love is than a fatted ox and hatred with It. V 17 .

= (Prv 17:1, AMP) =

Better is a dry morsel with quietness than a house full of feasting (on offered sacrifice) with strife.

= (Prv 16:8, AMP) =

Better is a little with righteousness(uprightness in every area and relation and right standing with God) than great revenue with injustice.

= (Prv 20:23, AMP) =

Diverse and deceitful weights are shamefully vile and abhorrent to the Lord, and false scales are not good.

Contentment with godliness is a great gain indeed. People become desperate to getting rich and richer not just because they are poor, but because they're not satisfied with what they have, so they desire excessively and rather than pursuing riches in the godly and rightful ways they prefer making it far quicker than their legal meanses and capacity of paces to getting rich and richer. In the essence of desiring immoderate fast wealth the desperate people despise the divine demand for living contentedly, but those who despise greed, desperation and illicitly fast gotten riches, and live a life of contentment are typically models of righteous living by contentment by moderate desires.

iii = SHUNNING TO EMULATE PROSPEROUS SINNERS =
(Prv 23:16-17, AMP).

Let not your heart envy sinners, but continue in the reverent and worshipful fear of the Lord all the day long. V 17. For surely there is a later end (a future and a reward) , and your hope and expectation shall not be cut off.

= (Prv 24:1-2, KJV) =

Be thou not envious against evil men, neither desire to be with them . V 1. For their heart studieth destruction, and their lips talk of mischief. V 2 .

SUPPORTING TEXT = (Ps 1:1; Ps 37:16; Isa 5:22; Hab 2:6; Luke 21:24; Rom 13:13; Eph 5:11,18; 1 Tim 6:6-10;

Some times while the righteous watch sinners prospering financially and materials wise, at the same time the ungodly wallowing in Sensuality, and the righteous thereby begin to envy and jealous the prosperous ungodly people, wondering why them the righteous will keep waiting and working patiently in godly manner and their full prosperity and success stay delayed, and those who don't honour God make it quickly and enjoy pleasures, the righteous will definitely loose focus from true godliness with this kind of mindset. That is why the above texts and the supporting texts are given to guide people on restraining from envy and jealousy toward the prospering godless and desiring to be like or better then them. But the righteous to keep working vigorously and waiting on God for satisfying their needs whether we become immensely financial and materials wealthy, moderate or poor, our faith is meant to cling on the principles of ever godliness and shun desire desperation which is evidenced by envying and emulating the supposed prospering ungodly.

There are other desires which must be moderated in humans lives, though not mentioned in the write up above, the key factors of this section of lessons are, there are lots of desires that life requires and there are lots of other lustful desires which are unnecessary to proper living. In whichever cases righteousness of God is a divine requisite in humans life and affairs, hence God demands that all humans should be disciplined pertaining to cravings and thereby moderate craving of anything, not craving lustfully but contentedly and rightfully to satisfy needs and not to gratify wants.

DESIRING ALCOHOLLIC CONSUMPTION = (Prv 23:20-21, AMP).

Do not associate with wine bibbers; be not among them nor among glutinous eaters of meat. V 20 . For the drunkard and the glutton shall come to poverty, and drowsiness shall clothes a man with rags. V 21.

= (Prov 23:31-35, ESV) =

[31] Do not look at wine when it is red, when it sparkles in the cup and goes down smoothly. [32] In the end it bites like a serpent and stings like an adder. [33] Your eyes will see strange things, and your heart utter perverse things. [34] You will be like one who lies down in the midst of the sea, like one who lies on the top of a mast. [35] "They struck me," you will say, "but I was not hurt; they beat me, but I did not feel it. When shall I awake? I must have another drink.

There have being trending controversies among different peoples over drinking of alcoholic drinks. Some say that, drinking alcohol is a sin, while some counter state against it by saying, that drinking alcohol is not a sin. Then one other fascinating matter that is risen from these controversies is; whom among those justifying drinking of alcohol and it's condemners are right. Some vindicate moderate drinking of alcohol while some others condemn it totally. Nevertheless; moderate and disciplined way of drinking alcohol can be right, and excess of it wrong. The issue at hand demands that, while seeking for pleasures and comfort that include pleasing life and appetite by drinking the pleasure seekers must seek it with diligence, which should be exemplified by refraining from such activities and associates that are capable of leading and victimising people through consistent heavy drinking of alcohol and thereby the victims are stupefied and in some occasions fail to focus on their life required responsibilities and ethical lifestyle which are to be their personal foundations for success. And the immoral pleasures as exemplified by excess drinking of alcohol, negligence of proper duties resulted from over sensuality and despising true ethics of life and ventures decode sins and attract, financial, spiritual/ moral poverty, and good health and life span breaching. Hence the wise should endeavour to receive the grace of God for self discipline and diligence and therefore moderate their quests for alcohol consumption and all other ungodly pleasures and comfort in order to express righteous living by moderation, in the sight of God. Drinking of alcohol or drinking it in excess begins from desiring it just as doing many other things begins from desiring it.

iv = MODERATING EATING DESIRE = (Prv 17:1, KJV).

Better is a dry morsel, and quietness therewith, than an house full of sacrifices with strife.

= (Prv 23:1-3,6-8, NAS) =

When you sit down to dine with a ruler, consider carefully what is before you. V 1 . And put a knife to your throat if, you ate a man of great appetite. V 2. Do not desire his delicacies for it us deceptive food. V 3. Do not eat the bread of a selfish man or desire his delicacies. V 6 For as he thinks within himself so he us, he says to you; eat and drink but his heart is not with you. V 7. You will vomit all the morsel you have eaten and waste all your compliments. 8

Like the previous like the recent= while seeking to please life and enjoy comfort the seekers should not be careless and carried away by the enticements of what they eat. Excessive eating is a sin while eating moderately is righteousness, and no one can eat moderately unless the eater is self disciplined over his or her appetite for food, and therefore eat with diligence regardless of great hunger, circumstances, free and pretended offer of free foods. Having done so God will be please and vindicates the moderate eaters as people of righteousness by desire and consumption. Moreover: by moderating the desire to eating the prudent can discern some of the traps and dangers that are attached to enticing foods offered to them and to dodge the dangers just by refusing to eat those foods.

v = MODERATING SEXUAL DESIRE = (Prv 5:3-8, AMP).

For the lips of a loose woman drop honey as a honeycomb, and her mouth is smoother than oil. V 3. But in the end she is bitter as wormwood, sharp as two edged and devouring sword. V 4. Her feet go down to death; her steps take hold of sheol (Hades, the place of death) V 5. She loses sight of and walk not in the path of life; her ways wind about aimlessly, and you cannot know them. V 6. Now Therefore my son, listen to me and depart not from the word of of my mouth. V 7. Let your way in life be far from her, and come not near the door of her house (avoid the very scenes of temptation.

Let your fountain(of human life) be blessed (with the rewards of fidelity) , and rejoice in the wife of your youth. V 18 . Let her be as loving hind and pleasant doe(tender, gentle attractive) let her bosom satisfy you at all times, and always be transported with delight in her love. V 19. Why should you, my son, be infatuated with a loose woman, embrace the bosom of and outsider, and go astray. V 20 .

SUPPORTING TEXTS = Prv 6:23-26; Prv chapter 7; Prv 9:13-18; Ps 19:8; Ps 109:105; Ezek 20:30; Col 2:8-10; 2 Pet 2:14-17; Rom 16:17; 1 Thes 5:19-22.

Contentment is not only about refraining from materials greed. It implies to all aspects of life, including contentment over sex. Without contentment moderation is impossible. For this, it is necessary that people should be absolutely self disciplined and not to have sex while they're unmarried, practice monogamy and keep enjoying the one and only legally marriage and sex partner of each married individual. Regardless of how enticing any man or woman that is not divinely official wife or husband of any person can be. God wills to subject all people to the prohibition of having romance, emotional and practical sex with anybody unmarried to them, and it costs self discipline to moderate the desire over sex by focusing on personal married life/sex partner or staying without sex when not married. Righteousness is justifiable through absolute restraint from sexual infidelity and moderate sex which is evident in focusing on personal marriage and soul mate for sexual pleasure and comfort.

*vi = **MODERATING AMBITIONS AND ADVENTURES =** (Prv 24:27, KJV).*

Prepare thy work without and make it fit for thy self in the field; and afterwards build thine house.

= (Prv 27:23-27, KJV) =

Be thou diligent to know the state of thy flocks, and look well to thy herds. V 23. For riches are not forever: And doth the crown endure to every generation. V 24. The hay appeareth and the tender grass sheweth itself. V 25. The lambs are for thy clothing, and the goats are the price of the field. V 26. And thou shalt have goats' milk enough for thy food, for the food of thy household and for the maintenance of thy maidens. V 27.

Some people mistakingly and sinfully, in their desires and quests for comfort and pleasures, feel reluctant and neglect their suppose prior tasks which are centralised in doing true works of God and proper personal works. Some people even despise their prior mandates completely, being carried by nonsensical pleasures and comforts while some people live their lives in opposite manner compared to the reluctant and negligent entities. However: It is proper that people should take their rightful obligations as priorities and engage themselves into labour, ensuring that; they're not engulfed by careless pleasures and comfort but being diligent and doing the right things they are to do and at the right times, afterwards seek, get and enjoy moderate and righteous pleasures and comfort in the Lord. Even at the beginning of desiring to venture and succeed then become great, the desire must be moderated and after the success the celebration must also be moderate to stay within the boundaries of self discipline and not to transgress and suffer for it.

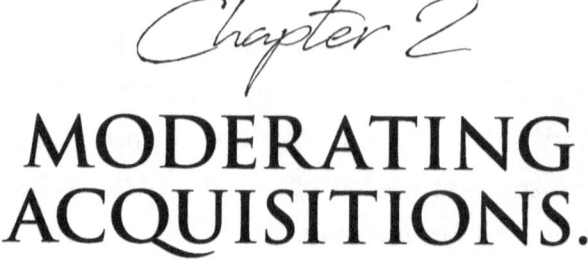

MODERATING ACQUISITIONS.

DEFINITION = The act of setting good boundaries to getting things in order to not commit offenses, crimes and sins while seeking and getting whatever.

MEMORY VERSE = *1 Tim 6:11 AMP = [11] But as for you, O man of God, flee from these things; aim at and pursue righteousness [true goodness, moral conformity to the character of God], godliness [the fear of God], faith, love, steadfastness, and gentleness. [2 Tim 3:17]*

INTRODUCTION

Moderating everything without compromising them is the fundamental factor to making contentment a reality, in the sense that anyone can desire to be contented in one or in all things and confess his or her righteous desire with rigour but cannot really achieve it due to his or her inability to discipline himself or herself over each of all things. Moderation is also the fundamental factor for self discipline while self discipline is a manifestation of outward contentment. Anybody as I said earlier can claim to be contented but may not even understand his or her state of character. Most selfish and greedy people don't know they're selfish and greedy in different ways, likewise most of those who are desperate to getting whatever they want, because they're all being driven by their lustful desires. But their character reveals their selfishness and greed. But as such can be contented for real only if they can moderate their desires and adventures and discipline themselves toward everything so they should not be crossing the boundary in doing and getting anything and to be comfortable with whatever they get with principles of diligence at any time while they continue to strive for excellence.

Moderation and self discipline which produce the reality of contentment are required in every facets of life.

> *Jms 2:10-11 AMP = [10] For whoever keeps the whole Law but stumbles in one point, he has become guilty of [breaking] all of it. [11] For He who said, "Do not commit adultery," also said, "Do not murder." Now if you do not commit adultery, but you murder, you have become guilty of transgressing the [entire] Law. [Ex 20:13, 14; Deut 5:17, 18]*

---

i = NOT AGITATING TOWARDS UNSCRUPULOUS THRIVING PEOPLE = (Prv 3:31, AMP).

Do not resentfully and be jealous of an unscrupulous man, and choose none of his ways.

Due to lust of the flesh and lust of the eyes people are prone to envy the unrighteous but prosperous people, though the envy which triggers jealousy in the enviers are not always against material prosperity of the wicked, but against their immorality, and their imagination that God can be partial against them (the righteous but mediocres) for not prospering them like or more than the unrighteous people.

At times, rather than to totally condemn and abhor the immoral behaviour of the ungodly; others who strive to live righteously begin pondering on why should they the God fearers exhibit self denials concerning desperation to be wealthy and concerning bodily sinful life, while they are poor to watch the ungodly swim in illicit wealthiness and sensual pleasures. As a reason, the supposedly righteous begin desiring to engage themselves into the pursuit of illicit wealth and enjoying various sinfully emotional and practical activities and pleasures, while renouncing their covenant relationship with God who had called them out from the darkness(illegality, occultism and sensuality) of this world into his marvellous light (true godliness).

From the contents of the text, we are warned to be self disciplined towards the ungodly rich and their carnal pleasures, because we prove to be carnally minded if we are being distracted and uncomfortable by the ungodly, their fortunes and pleasures. But controlling our material desires, consumption and emotional appetites defines our state of being truly contented in the Lord. We the righteous are also to have the understanding that there are some other ways God prosper his own outside of material wealth and we should channel our attention and pursuit toward those immaterial areas of prosperity with the willingness to pay the genuine costs for attracting God's favour to having them.

ii = DESPISING EVIL PROSPEROUS COMPANY = (Prov 4:1-2, KJV).

Be thou not envious against evil men, neither desire to be with them. For their heart studieth destruction, And their lips talk of mischief.

While we are moved by the prosperity of the wicked then we envy them, we should as well consider their mischievous mindsets through which they acquire most of their wealth and pleasures. Also their mischievous mindsets with which the prosperous wicked are yet to damage the lives and fortunes of others for their own self gratification. While considering the negative consequences of the prosperous wicked, we are clarified that, we are forbidden to share companionship with them in evil adventures no matter how much dividends they can offer, as true people of God we're meant to be. Being contented in the Lord , then becomes apparent in our ability to restrain from the companies of the prosperous wicked and despise the prosperous wicked themselves. Whoever rejects Satan must also reject his activities and offers.

iii = MAINTAINING PEACE WITH GOD = (Ps 37:1).

Fret not thyself because of evil doers, Neither be thou envious against the workers of iniquity. (KJV) .

The psalmist call the unscrupulous people, evildoers, because they are known with evil activities, he also call them workers of iniquity, because all of their ungodly activities are rebellions towards God's will and commands. We are therefore to be continually self conscious about how we selfishly approach the assumingly prosperous worldly people. And we must always be satisfied with whatever God gives us every moment, while we remain happy in the situations we find ourselves for God's sake and his glory, and for our own peace. To be and remain obedient to God and sustaining our covenant relationship with him is a relevant reason of consideration for living a contented life.

iv = EXERCISING GODLY PATIENCE = (Ps 73:2-7 AMP).

[2] But as for me, my feet came close to stumbling, My steps had almost slipped. [3] For I was envious of the arrogant As I saw the prosperity of the wicked. [4] For there are no pains in their death, Their body is fat and pampered. [5] They are not in trouble as other men, Nor are they plagued like mankind. [6] Therefore pride is their necklace; Violence covers them like a garment [like a long, luxurious robe]. [7] Their eye bulges from fatness [they have more than the heart desires]; The imaginations of their mind run riot [with foolishness].

The psalmist testified in the first verse of this scripture on how he was almost swept along while he was envying the prosperous workers of iniquity. Some of the reasons the psalmist considered, then began envying the ungodly were their threat of death, physical violence and intimidating pride of the ungodly rich exhibit against others, While seeing all of the potency of the prosperous wicked the psalmist was perplexed, and was nearly carried away, but by God's grace he the psalmist was able to control himself from wondering about how the wicked seem to be more prosperous than the righteous, because the psalmist could comprehend that, what seem prosperous but out of the track of true godliness are fake and temporal, but the righteous must be patient with God and in God , so to say. The righteous through godly patience learns to be contented in the Lord, working wisely and consistently and waiting for God's own time and methods for elevating him. The psalmist is a model to any other person who can improve his or her life of contentment by being patient with God.

v = ABHORRING BRIBERY = (Prv 15:27, NAS).

He who profits illicitly, troubles his own house, But he who hates bribes will live.

The illicit profiteers deliberately or ignorantly cause themselves household and generational calamities, Because a man reaps equivalence of the kinds of seeds he sows. Though there are always humans shrewdness being displayed to escape from the repercussions of extortion, yet the extortionists definitely pay for the evil of deprivation they commit against others, meanwhile the extortionists would be free from reciprocal calamities if, they had shunned their greediness that leads them to engaging in false means of gaining mostly by bribery. In paradox; The man of godly contentment truly abhors and despises taking bribe, because he is always satisfied in the Lord with God's providence for him at any point in time, knowing that the Omnipotent God will never fail to suffice him with daily life's necessities. By pondering on God's efficacy to constantly provide, the contented people of God, refuse to collect financial, material bribes and ungodly favour to vindicate the unjust then condemn the just and deprive them of their legal entitlements. From all that have been said here: it is clear that, abhorring and shunning bribery is an approved evidence of being contented in the Lord, as we know that bribery is a rebellion to God's law of protecting humans rights, lives and properties.

vi = CONDUCTING A FAIR LEADERSHIP = (Prv 29:4, NAS).

The king gives stability to the land by justice, But a man who takes bribe overthrows it.

Bribery and corruption is a key factor to the instabilities of national, international and domestic province economy, peace and tranquillity. Because though the bribe givers and bribe collectors are favoured and highly enriched, their peace and tranquillity are not guaranteed, due to human retaliation from those they humiliate and deprive of their belongings and in most occasion divine vengeance upon the corrupt puts our domains in chaos. Moreover breach of trust results in from bribery. The bribes givers will soon cease to trust those they bribe, as the bribe givers believe that, the bribery collectors will as well, someday collect bribes from others to betray them who previously bribe them against others.

In the same vein the bribe collectors themselves will loose their trust on their bribers, as the bribe collectors will believe that, their bribe givers will someday bribe others against them, let alone the deprived developing a chronic hate and distrust toward both the givers and receivers of bribes.

Nevertheless; there are still wise leaders with integrity who ensures that their leadership domains constantly stay peaceful, regardless of the oppositions that challenge them for doing so. The wise leaders of all categories pursue justice of the land not because they don't know the values of money and favours; But because, they are contented with such which God pleasingly provides for them, while they understand the repercussions of indulging in bribery, then forbid it. Thus the abhorrence of bribery by the wise discloses righteousness by being contented in the Lord.

*vii = **SHUNNING SELF CENTEREDNESS** = (Isah 5:8 AMP).*

Woe (judgment is coming) to those who join house to house and join field to field [to increase their holdings by depriving others], Until there is no more room [for others], So that you have to live alone in the midst of the land!

The greedy are hereby cursed with disgrace and reproach, Because they are eager to have it all alone and dominate others, The self centered greedy are grieved for seeing others prospering, They desire that every good thing should be theirs alone. They can kill and maim others to ensure that, no one matches them in wealth, powers, positions and status. It's not in the political setups alone, the greedy do the same even in the Christian churches and other religious entities, in business and factories sectors. But godly contentment is an evidential righteousness in the lives of those who desire that others should prosper the same way they do, And never bother themselves even when others happen to be more prosperous, than them. Prophet Isaiah is a model of the selflessly contented person in this respect.

*viii = **SHUNNING ALL MEANS OF ILLICIT WEALTH** = [Jer 17:11 AMP].*

[11] "Like the partridge that hatches eggs which she has not laid, So is he who makes a fortune in ways that are unjust. It will be lost to him before his days are over, And in the end he will be [nothing but] a fool."

The text reveals, how illicit profiteering eventually stupefy its subjects, And that is because, the desperate extortionists, invest much of their labours in cheating others to be uniquely wealthy; But the nemesis of their illegal acquisition makes them restless and in most incidents send them to early grave, while they leave all of their greedily acquired wealth to some other people whom they would never imagined partaking from their sinful labour for richness. Prophets Jeremiah rebuked his contemporaries who were getting wealth by all criminal means possible. Meanwhile apostle Paul warns and advises that the church and all humans should live the life of contentment with godliness to avoid all of the miserable consequences of indulging in all kinds of criminality for accumulating wealth.

Knowing all these; the godly wise are expected to be contented at all times and in all circumstances, in Order to not offend God and man and suffers the consequences of their extortion at last. Moreover: the godly wise should exhibit righteousness by contentment as a righteousness to retain his integrity and honour in the Lord, While the sinners are to learn to live like the righteous.

ix = JETTISONNING THE PATH OF THE BARBARIANS =
(Prov 4:14-15 AMP).

[14] Do not enter the path of the wicked, And do not go the way of evil men. [15] Avoid it, do not travel on it; Turn away from it and pass on. [16] For the wicked cannot sleep unless they do evil; And they are deprived of sleep unless they make someone stumble and fall. [17] For they eat the bread of wickedness And drink the wine of violence.

We are forewarned to permanently stay clear from the company and systems of the barbarians whose hobby is to antagonise others and rob them, then spend much time in celebrating and pleasuring in the loots of their barbarity. We are forewarned to shun barbarians and their ways because, their activities are absolutely evil and transgression of God's law of love and protection.

Without greediness people will not engage themselves in barbarity. It is the desperation to acquiring materials, greatness and fulfilment that lure people into such an act. But being contented in the Lord, restricts the wise to not desire and venture in barbarism, as the godly wise know that, barbarism is a crime against God and humanity, But God is pleased with those who are always satisfied with what they have at any moment then righteously endeavour to have more rather than getting them by violence. The ability to avoid barbarity and stay contented in the Lord is righteousness of acquisition moderation, that secures approval for the upright in God's sight.

x = DESPISING DESPERATE DESIRES AND VENTURING =
(Prv 16:19, KJV).

It is better to be humble in spirit than to divide the spoil with the proud.

Without spiritual and emotional humility contentment is unattainable. That is why we are hereby persuaded to be self humbled concerning our cravings for possessions, mostly while dealing with some; proudly, arrogant and desperate money/ wealth mongers. By the time we are able to control ourselves toward financial and material acquisition, without being told, the public will begin to discern our righteousness by moderate aspirations, ambitions and acquisition, while God in the spirit already understands our endeavour to moderate our cravings, he will then mark it on our behaves as righteousness.

x = WORKING MODERATELY AND SMARTLY = (Prv 23:4, NAS).

Do not weary yourself to gain wealth, Cease from your consideration of it.

Too many people who aspire to be rich and great exhaust themselves working so hard and without ordeal never get rich and great, just because they work excessively but not smartly. Some of such a people believe that their getting rich and great is tied to how much labour they invest. But in reality it's not about how much of the quantities but how well the qualities and benefits. The effort to getting rich and great by so much labour also triggers anxiety and desperation for accomplishing so many things, and it deprives each of its subject of his or her contentment, though that does not guarantee the desired riches and elevation. At times some people who work vigorously and smartly don't become rich and great due to any negative reason, while some others who do the same thing are rich and great. Working moderately and smartly does not imply that anybody should embrace mediocre labour and mediocre results. But it implies that we all should be labouring wisely and excellently but should not overwhelm ourselves with labour and we should not be anarchic while labouring and we should not be anarchic while we might have laboured diligently but could not get rich and great. Rather we should be adaptive to excellent, mediocre and poor success only on the condition of we have done all the right things we should do for achieving excellence and have it or could not have it.

*xi = **PREFERING PEACE TO TROUBLES = (Prov 15:16-17 KJV).***

[16] Better is little with the fear of the LORD Than great treasure and trouble therewith. [17] Better is a dinner of herbs where love is, Than a stalled ox and hatred therewith.

= (Prov 16:8 KJV) =

[8] Better is a little with righteousness Than great revenues without right.

= (Prv 22:28, KJV) =

Remove not the ancient mark, which your fathers have set Up.

It doesn't matter the financial and general material poverty you are experiencing. It doesn't matter whether all your mates had made it in life while you're the only one remaining. God's word and commands remain the same yester years, present and future years.

The word of God reveals that desperation to acquiring wealth is a proof of greed. Our predicaments are not acceptable excuses to infringing God's law of contentment; Rather we are to constantly obey God's law, while depending on him for our higher greatness through his provisions. But whether God gives us little or great possessions we are not to be bothered about it, Because God will suffice us with our essential needs as long as we keep on walking and working with him diligently. So stressing our lives for not having enough or more than abundance or because of others who possess more than us at the moment is irrelevant, as it shows our in undisciplined cravings. But being contented always with godliness is a justified righteousness of moderation. Peace with little possessions is more important than troubles with great possessions. The wise go for peace with little possessions, aspiring and working for peace with abundance and superabundance.

xii = **PROTECTING PERSONAL INTEGRITY = (Prov 30:7-9 AMP).**

[7] Two things I have asked of You; Do not deny them to me before I die: [8] Keep deception and lies far from me; Give me neither poverty nor riches; Feed me with the food that is my portion, [9] So that I will not be full and deny You and say, "Who is the Lord?" Or that I will not be poor and steal, And so profane the name of my God. [Deut 8:12, 14, 17; Neh 9:25, 26; Job 31:24; Hos 13:6].

SUPPORTING TEXT = 1st Tim 6:6-10.

Here the bible commentator prayed to God to bless him with the spirit of contentment, which forbids greed, lies and deception which the greed incurs. Spirit of contentment is the fundamental factor to shunning greed and desperate ventures to getting rich.

There is nothing wrong with having abundant wealth with godliness; But rather than being carried away by weight of glory from wealth whereby the children of God defile their godliness and abuse God's name and majesty, they (God's a children) will be better having just their daily bread (sufficiency) if that will be the criteria to remain contented in the Lord.

Nevertheless; Abject poverty is another dangerous weapon the enemies use to lure God believers into stealing and other duplicity, whereby God's people transgress over God's law of contentment.

With this clue, the wise in the Lord must pray and work seriously in order to prosper beyond poverty level while they live in obedience to God's word and engage themselves in licit ventures. Moreso to be matured in handling riches and splendours in godliness.

*xiii = **DEVELOPING REAL SENSE OF SUERIORITY = (Ps 27:16).***

A little that a righteous man hath is better than the riches of many wicked.

Considering fact that, desperation to getting rich lure its victims into unwarranted temptations, and understanding that there are great differences between our wants and our needs, we will be able to be self controlled in our ventures to acquire wealth.

Being desperate to get rich is an effort to getting into, frustration, losing focus from godliness and to resort in worldliness.

Christians should be wise enough to shun greed of all kinds, more especially the lust to acquiring money. By so doing our righteousness of contentment will be obvious before God and man and our Christian integrity and dignity remain intact. Above all we must no more be feeling timid and being intimidated by the ungodly rich people with their ostentatious display of their achievements and splendour. But we should develop godly boldness with our realisation of the truth that one with God is greater and a majority. We are therefore far more valuable if we have little with godliness than the licit and illicit rich people whose covenant relationship with God is broken and shattered.

While the ungodly rich are gallivanting with their wealth giving the impression that they have risen above all the poor and middle class people, we the Christians with integrity and virtuous treasures must be evaluating ourselves and the ungodly from God's own evaluation. For this we should be liberated from our mental subjugation which forces us to conceive the fallacy of we being inferior to those rich people who have no godly integrity and other godly internal valuables. Doing this makes the contented people to be formidable, resilient and consistent with the little or great possessions with contentment.

Chapter 3

MODERATING CONSUMPTION.

DEFINITION = It's the ability to be diligent in eating drinking, having sex, inhaling and smoking substances in order to not abuse the edibles / consumables or the consumers abusing themselves by consumption.

The ability to discern benefits and consequences of desired foods and drinks, and other consumables and to consume them with the right purposes and limits.

MEMORY VERSES = *(Prov 25:16, ESV).*

> *If you have found honey, eat only enough for you, lest you have your fill of it and vomit it.*

> *= (Prov 31:4-5, ESV) =*

> *It is not for kings, O Lemuel, it is not for kings to drink wine, or for rulers to take strong drink, [5] lest they drink and forget what has been decreed and pervert the rights of all the afflicted.*

> *= (Rom 12:1 ESV) =*

> *I appeal to you therefore, brothers, by the mercies of God, to present your bodies as a living sacrifice, holy and acceptable to God, which is your spiritual worship.*

INTRODUCTION

Eating, drinking, smoking, inhaling and sex habits are serious issue that, Christians are supposed to be well concerned about. Because many at times, Christians carelessly eat, drink, smoke / inhale and have sex unethically and thereby abuse what they consume, and themselves who consume them. Ignorance of godly ethics about consumption keeps so many Christian in obscure that, excessive and improper ways of eating, drinking, smoking / inhaling having sex with anybody or anything is a sin. However: there are Christians who are aware of the sin of immodest consumption yet are unable to overcome it, while there are some other Christians who are aware of it and have overcome it. The cases is the same with the non Christians among whom some are ignorant, some are aware but weak and some aware overcomers. It is very common to see most nominal Christians who strive to justify their immoderate alcoholism, inhaling and smoking of intoxicating drugs with the logic that, after all Jesus turned water into wine, some strive to justify their smoking of Marijuana leaves, cigarettes and other intoxicating drug but smokeless with the logic that, all that they smock are made with natural vegetables and other things created by God. But do all the logic the immoderate consumers apply really justify them? Are all of their logics in line with God's principles for consumption? As I usually say; God's laws and principles are unchangeable, so whatever acts which include consumption manners that contradict God's approved way of consumption are sins. It doesn't matter whom the consumer may be, what really matter is the sure word of God that must be obeyed.

And be blessed as the righteous by consumption or disobey and bear the consequences of disobeying God's word starting from here on earth and to eternity if there is no repentance in the process of lives of the immoderate consumers. Regardless of all that have been said: The principled Christians dare to show forth their righteousness by being careful to accept whatever they eat and drink, and never to inhale or smoke any polluting substance ensuring they are not carried away to consume abusively.

BEING SATISFIED WITH GOD PROVIDED FOOD = (Prv 15:17, KJV).

Better is a dinner of herb, where love is, than a stalled ox and hatred therewith.

= (Prv 17:1, KJV) =

Better is a dry morsel, And quietness therewith, Than an house full of sacrifices with strife.

The inability of most people to live within the means of God's provision of food for them is an evidence of greed which oblige them to be eating excessively, abusing God's glory for providing the food, rebelling against God's law for consumption moderation. Eve and Adam are the primal examples of the greedily immoderate consumers, who suffered for the retribution of greedy consumption.

= (Gen 3:6-7 ESV) =

[6] So when the woman saw that the tree was good for food, and that it was a delight to the eyes, and that the tree was to

be desired to make one wise, she took of its fruit and ate, and she also gave some to her husband who was with her, and he ate. [7] Then the eyes of both were opened, and they knew that they were naked. And they sewed fig leaves together and made themselves loincloths.

Unlike Eve and Adam, consumption moderation, saves us of the painful retribution that befall the greedy eaters. Each of us had been eating any kind of food / fruit excessively and being spinning thereby but the acceptance of Jesus salvation and the knowledge of God's rules for Being moderate with whatever we eat has reformed some of us humans to become disciplined with eating while some fail to be disciplined even though they have the knowledge, and some are immoderate eaters because they're ignorant of the God required moderate eating of every food and fruit. We can maintain our peace and opportunities with God to some extent only by eating with self discipline and never to cross the boundaries of the food which God gives us.

BEING DILIGENT WITH EATING FOOD GIFTS = (Prov 23:1-3, 6-8 ESV) =

[1] When you sit down to eat with a ruler, observe carefully what is before you, [2] and put a knife to your throat if you are given to appetite. [3] Do not desire his delicacies, for they are deceptive food. [6] Do not eat the bread of a man who is stingy; do not desire his delicacies, [7] for he is like one who is inwardly calculating. "Eat and drink!" he says to you, but his heart is not with you. [8] You will vomit up the morsels that you have eaten, and waste your pleasant words.

It is important we should be diligent to accepting food as gifts from people. I'm not denying the fact that there are people of good will who give food freely to others, but I'm pointing to the fact that there are other sets of people who are aristocrats, some other upper class people who use their affluence and influence to lure many people into accepting food gifting from them while they (the influential) have some ulterior motives. Some middle and low class people like the upper class do the same thing against others. Some people give supposed free food to others with the intention of buying their support for executing some functions of the givers. Most African politicians use food to buy the conscience of many of the voters and other citizens who support them to win elections but the politicians never really have the wellbeing of the citizens at heart. Some young men use food to lure some young women into having immoral sex with them. Some people are initiated into some occultic kingdoms through food gifting. Some of the occultists use food gifting to steal destinies of some of their beneficiaries.

So besides offending God and suffering for it: People who are not careful with collecting foods from others and eating them can get themselves, their destinies including their lives into some jeopardies. Which means the careless consumers of food gifts are probable to become victims of evil but generous givers of food. The proverbialist warns we should be precautious to receiving free food from people, considering that there are people who are manipulative through giving of free food to others, so that the precautious should prevent themselves from victimisation. You're not under obligation to accept and eat free foods but you're under obligation to be widely selective with collecting and eating foods from others.

EATING WITH PURPOSES = (Prov 25:16 ESV).

If you have found honey, eat only enough for you, lest you have your fill of it and vomit it.

We must learn to be regular with being purposeful with what we eat no matter how good they may be. Some people observe the principle of purposeful eating while others do not. Those who observe the principle in question eat whatever with the intention of getting the benefits of the foods and maintain their boundaries with the quantities they eat, and never compete with anybody in the eating and so to prevent themselves from abusing the foods and consumption self abuses. Honey is used in the bible passage as a reference food to guide us to realise the importance of eating it moderately to settle hunger and not to eat it excessively after the hunger has been settled and eating it the more just for fulfilling a lustfully greedy appetite for it.

Honey as mentioned in the text, is a symbol of sweet and nutritious food, which its taste and functions make it special and very attractive for consumption. Regardless of the uniqueness of honey as an example, we are hereby instructed to be self controlled over our appetite and desire to eat any kind of food mostly our delighted special food and not be carried away by the speciality of the food we are so much attracted to, and thereby abuse our selves and defile our bodies which are God's living temples in the process of excessive eating. We should as well comprehend that excessive eating of any thing is a sin. Furthermore: we must moderate our eating habits irrespective of how our lustful appetites may drive us. By moderating our eating life , our righteousness by consumption will be vivid, And we will be regarded as decent consumers both by God and man.

AVOIDING DRINKING OF ALCOHOL = (Prov 31:4-5 ESV).

[4] It is not for kings, O Lemuel, it is not for kings to drink wine, or for rulers to take strong drink, [5] lest they drink and forget what has been decreed and pervert the rights of all the afflicted.

The king in the bible passage represents a leader in every respect of endeavour, who is warned to not participate in alcohol consumption due to what he represents and the tasks at stake under his custody. Judging problematic matters between his communal fellows. For this reason if not for any other the king must have a clear eyes and mind althrough because he never can tell when a matter will be brought to him for judgement and he owes it to his people to attend to them without delay and always to pass a fair judgement. The king as a judge is also a warring defender of his people just like the Judges of ancient Israelites of which Samson, Jephthah and Gideon were examples. The law for avoidance of alcoholic consumption is a part of the law of Nazarene which was given to Samson even before his birth. I have not concluded that drinking alcohol moderately is a sin but there is an obligation to avoid it totally when God's need calls for it.

HAVING JOY AND HAPPINESS WITHOUT ALCOHOL = (Prov 31:6-7 ESV).

[6] Give strong drink to the one who is perishing, and wine to those in bitter distress; [7] let them drink and forget their poverty and remember their misery no more.

Most drunkards began that kind of life by looking for joy and happiness to relief themselves of agony, and in most cases drinking it excessively, never knowing that alcoholism is not the solution. The realisation of this fact compels anyone to restrict himself or herself from alcoholism. Some intelligent people who drink alcohol never depends on it to have their joy and happiness, so they are moderate with drinking it. Furthermore: By indulging in alcoholism some foolish people trivialise their own future and destiny, using their precious time, financial and natural resources for funs. So the kings which You and I are in some ways are warned to be moderate with drinking of alcohol and the best option is to avoid it completely, remembering that our own destinies and of those connected to us are at stake in the kind of life we choose to live. And we should be wise to securing our better future and destinies and that of others as much as we can deal with alcohol for actualising it.

DRINKING PURPOSEFULLY = (1ˢᵗ Tim 5:22-23 ESV).

[22] Do not be hasty in the laying on of hands, nor take part in the sins of others; keep yourself pure. [23] (No longer drink only water, but use a little wine for the sake of your stomach and your frequent ailments.)

Most Christian drinkers of alcohol strive to justify their consumption of it by quoting apostle Paul who made the comment in the bible passage. In reality Paul used his statement as a metaphor to motivate Timothy so he could upgrade in the Christian faith and spirituality and functions in righteousness, as a church leader who should be an excellent exemplar to the rest of the members. In addition to that, Paul asked Timothy and the rest to be taking little alcoholic drink to resolve their stomach problems all as a metaphorical comment. But most people interpret his statement as if a little alcohol without being mixed with some other things can cure stomach ache or whatever abdominal sickness to the full. Apostle Paul's metaphorical comment is intended to taking in the alcoholic drink for medication. But the deception of the self justified alcoholic Christians is the fact that they rarely drink it on medication purpose, but they drink it for appeasing their lustful appetite for it.

However: even if the apostle really means drinking of alcohol for curing stomach problems, any of the drinkers must drink it only when they have stomach problems and never to drink it when they don't have stomach problems, because drinking it for any ulterior motive is an abuse of it and it's a sin. Both the Christians who drink alcohol and all others who depend on this statement of apostle Paul to do so should understand they're obliged to be drinking it only for stomach problems. The same is applicable to all who smoke herbs , those who inject or inhale hard drugs. They should be taking them according to the purpose for which God has made them.

Chapter 4

MODERATING SEX LIFE.

DEFINITION.

MODERATING SEX LIFE = Is the ability to be contented with one and only life panther as a wife for a man or a husband for a woman, without having extramarital or premarital sex.

It Is the single people's ability to stay out of sex until they get married and be having sex only with their legally married partners.

It is the married people's ability to have sex only with their legally married partners all of their lives.

It is the ability to restrain from fornication and adultery.

It is the ability to repent from and quit from fornication and adultery, incest, homosexuality, and bestiality.

MEMORY VERSE = *1ˢᵗ Cor 6:18 ESV = [18] Flee from sexual immorality. Every other sin a person commits is outside the body, but the sexually immoral person sins against his own body.*

INTRODUCTION

While continuously pondering on financial and materials greediness, and desperation to acquiring them; We shouldn't forget that though sext is not substantial but emotional, yet, sex perversion is undeniably an evidence of desperation to acquire numerous sex partners, than one to one as God had instituted it from the time of his creation.

The Spirit of greedy acquisition is responsible for luring people into polygamy, and the controversy for justifying it. Our human ancestors including the Israelites of old were immensely polygamous and polyandrous not because it is the will of God but they did it through their lust for sex and their ignorance of The word and will of God.

Lust for sex led King Solomon of the bible to marry, seven hundred wives, hoarded three hundred concubines and other inumeric princesses. All that Solomon did with these numbers of women was to greedily acquire them to constantly satisfy his sexual lust and emotion.

Regardless of all these, the word, principles and will of God stand sure, and they are the foundation upon which true Christianity and godliness and all other realities of life are established. Any contradiction to Monogamy and total restraint from ungodly sex is a sin, But abiding to the principles of monogamy and restraint from sex perversion is a proven evidence of being contented with legally personal life and sex partners.

Even Jesus reveals that looking at women and men lustfully with sexual emotion is a sin of mental fornication and adultery.

It is discovered that, both the married and the unmarried alike constantly have carnal sex motives toward strange males and females(those they're not married to), And by lustfully imagining, attempting to or properly have illegal sex give clear evidence of desperation to acquiring much sex partners and indulging in sinful sex pleasures. But the contented in the Lord concerning sex dare to be self disciplined, as being Christian chaste, refraining from sex till they marry and keep having sex only with their God approved one marriage partner. The married then keeping to divine principle of monogamy and permanent restraining from illicit sex.

BEING CONTEND IN MONOGAMY = (Prov 5:18-20 ESV).

[18] Let your fountain be blessed, and rejoice in the wife of your youth, [19] a lovely deer, a graceful doe. Let her breasts fill you at all times with delight; be intoxicated always in her love. [20] Why should you be intoxicated, my son, with a forbidden woman and embrace the bosom of an adulteress?

This is an extortion for being pleased and satisfied with personal One and Only partner. Though the text directs the exhortation specifically to men, encouraging them to permanently be pleased and satisfied with their wives and never flirt around, the content of the said scripture, applies also to women endeavouring to be permanently pleased and satisfied with their husbands and never imagine or attempting flirting with other men.

The singles are herby also warned to have a stable patience and abstain from fornication until they are legally married, then each of them sticking to his or her own partner alone after as soon as they will be joined in marriage.

We are exhorted to be pleased with whatever shapes, colours and designs of breasts, hips and skins our wives possess, though God has several kinds of shapes and designs he had made among women; Men are to be self disciplined concerning sexual attractions from all other women, then focus on their individual wives alone and be satisfied with them in sex.

Married women and both the male and female singles are not exempted from the law of sex contentment with life partners, One individuals or one set of people are always used as examples to imparting comprehensive instructions to others. It is one thing to know that God wills we should be contented with our married partners concerning sex, But it is something very different to abide to the will of God concerning sex and marriage.

Knowing the will of God and transgressing it is a deliberate sin of indiscipline. But obeying the known will of God is righteousness of self discipline; So obeying the law of marriage and sex is righteousness of self discipline and contentment / moderation God's way.

King Solomon who made the statement of the scripture for this was a tremendous polygamists who suffered a great repercussion of it, then learnt his lessons through which he recognised the incomparability of polygamy to monogamy, exhorting that people should be moderate with sex and that should be only by monogamy.

REPENTING FROM SEXUAL IMMORALITY = (1st Cor 6:16-20 ESV).

[16] Or do you not know that he who is joined to a prostitute becomes one body with her? For, as it is written, "The two will become one flesh." [17] But he who is joined to the Lord becomes one spirit with him. [18] Flee from sexual immorality. Every other sin a person commits is outside the body, but the sexually immoral person sins against his own body. [19] Or do you not know that your body is a temple of the Holy Spirit within you, whom you have from God? You are not your own, [20] for you were bought with a price. So glorify God in your body.

God regards fornication and adultery with all other sex perversions as taboos.

Through the mouth of prophet apostle Paul God makes us to understand that, fornication and adultery are spiritual pollutants. No child of God will indulge in fornication and adultery and remain spiritually sound at all times, there is a liability for departure of the holy spirit from the lives of chronic sexual immorals, unless they truly repent, if not the holy spirit leaves their lives and never dwell in them anymore. For these reasons; Fornicators, adulterers and adulteresses are expected to properly repent and be converted, then begin to live the life of marriage and sex principles from the word of God, thus they become contented in the Lord by moderate sex. And it will count for their righteousness. Moreover: moderating sexual life helps for a progressive manifestation in the Christian ministry.

PROTECTING SACREDNESS OF THE CHURCH = (2nd Peter 2:14-15, 17 ESV)

[14] They have eyes full of adultery, insatiable for sin. They entice unsteady souls. They have hearts trained in greed. Accursed children! [15] Forsaking the right way, they have gone astray. They have followed the way of Balaam, the son of Beor, who loved gain from wrongdoing, [17] These are waterless springs and mists driven by a storm. For them the gloom of utter darkness has been reserved.

Not only that God is angry with immoral sex practitioners, he complains and laments concerning their unrepentance from it. God's complaint and lamentation over the sexual immorals is also because of how the immorals progress in seducing others and that escalates to promoting sexual immorality among the church. Therefore the wise in the Lord must endeavour to permanently abstain from immoral sex, to properly exhibit sexual contentment based on God's word. By doing so, God will be Glad and approves the observers of God's mandates for sex as being righteous in that aspect. Keeping the sanctity of the church intact must be a considerable factor for refraining from sexual immorality and like the church like all other organisations.

AVOIDING INCEST = (1st Cor 5:1 KJV)

[1] It is reported commonly that there is fornication among you, and such fornication as is not so much as named among the Gentiles, that one should have his father's wife.

Apostle Paul expresses his bitter cry over stepmother with stepson incest in addition to adultery and fornication that were celebrated by the church at Corinth.

= (Lev 18:6-7 NKJV) =

[6] 'None of you shall approach anyone who is near of kin to him, to uncover his nakedness: I am the Lord. [7] The nakedness of your father or the nakedness of your mother you shall not uncover. She is your mother; you shall not uncover her nakedness.

God through the mouth of Moses warned the ancient Israelites as soon as they settled in the promised land, that mother with son and all dimensions of incest must not be practiced among them.

Lev 18:8-10 =

Do not have sexual relations with any of your father's wives, for this would violate your father. "Do not have sexual relations with your sister or half sister, whether she is your father's daughter or your mother's daughter, whether she was born into your household or someone else's. "Do not have sexual relations with your granddaughter, whether she is your son's daughter or your daughter's daughter, for this would violate yourself.

As God continues through Moses: he warns against stepmother with stepson, half brother with half sister, grandfather with granddaughter committing incest.

Lev 18:11-17

Do not have sexual relations with your stepsister, the daughter of any of your father's wives, for she is your sister."

Never between half brothers and half sisters,

Do not have sexual relations with your father's sister, for she is your father's close relative. "Do not have sexual relations with your mother's sister, for she is your mother's close relative. "Do not violate your uncle, your father's brother, by having sexual relations with his wife, for she is your aunt."

Never between aunts and their nephews nor uncles with their nieces.

Do not have sexual relations with your daughter-in-law; she is your son's wife, so you must not have sexual relations with her.

Never between father-in-laws with daughters in-laws, nor between mother in-laws and son in-laws.

Do not have sexual relations with your brother's wife, for this would violate your brother. Do not have sexual relations with both a woman and her daughter.

Never between wives and their brother in-laws nor husbands with their sister in-laws.

And do not take her granddaughter, whether her son's daughter or her daughter's daughter, and have sexual relations with her. They are close relatives, and this would be a wicked act.

Never between uncles and stepdaughter in-laws nor aunts with stepson in-laws.

Protecting household sanctity, prestige, dignity and integrity with worshipping God in holiness are the major factors for the divine warnings regarding incest.

Deut 27:20

Cursed is anyone who has sexual intercourse with one of his father's wives, for he has violated his father.' And all the people will reply, 'Amen.

Incest is a cursed act and those who participate in it are also cursed.

Lev 20:11 = If a man has sexual relations with his father's wife, he has dishonoured his father. Both the man and the woman are to be put to death; their blood will be on their own heads.

Death penalty for stepmother with stepson or stepfather with stepdaughter incest.

Lev 20:12 =

If a man has sexual relations with his daughter-in-law, both of them are to be put to death. What they have done is a perversion; their blood will be on their own heads.

Death penalty for father in-laws with daughter in-laws or mother in-laws with son in-laws incest.

Lev 20:14 =

If a man marries both a woman and her mother, he has committed a wicked act. The man and both women must be burned to death to wipe out such wickedness from among you.

Death penalty for man with mother and daughter in marriage or woman with father and son in marriage.

Lev 20:19-21

Do not have sexual relations with your aunt, whether your mother's sister or your father's sister. This would dishonour a close relative. Both parties are guilty and will be punished for their sin. "If a man has sex with his uncle's wife, he has violated his uncle. Both the man and woman will be punished for their sin, and they will die childless.

Death penalty with childlessness for aunts with stepsons or uncles with their stepdaughters incest.

If a man marries his brother's wife, it is an act of impurity. He has violated his brother, and the guilty couple will remain childless.

Childlessness for brother in-laws with their brothers's wives or vice versa.

2ⁿᵈ Sam 13:7-14

So David agreed and sent Tamar to Amon's house to prepare some food for him. When Tamar arrived at Amnon's house, she went to the place where he was lying down so he could watch her mix some dough. Then she baked his favourite dish for him. But when she set the serving tray before him, he refused to eat. "Everyone get out of here," Amnon told his servants. So they all left. Then he said to Tamar, "Now bring the food into my bedroom and feed it to me here." So Tamar took his favorite dish to him. 11 But as she was feeding him, he grabbed her and demanded, "Come to bed with me, my darling sister." "No, my brother!" she cried. "Don't be foolish! Don't do this to me! Such wicked things aren't done in Israel. Where could I go in my shame? And you would be called one of the greatest fools in Israel. Please, just speak to the king about it, and he will let you marry me." But Amnon wouldn't listen to her, and since he was stronger than she was, he raped her.

Amnon by rape, sexually abused his half sister Tamar who was Absalom's full sister, and in a furious revenge Absalom murdered him.

Gen 35:22

While he was living there, Reuben had intercourse with Bilhah, his father's concubine, and Jacob soon heard about it. These are the names of the twelve sons of Jacob:

Gen 49:4

But you are as unruly as a flood, and you will be first no longer. For you went to bed with my wife; you defiled my marriage couch.

Reuben committed incest with Bilhah, one of his fathers young wives and his father angrily cursed him and his descendants with subordinate servitude to their co Jacobite descendants.

Ezek 22:9-10

People accuse others falsely and send them to their death. You are filled with idol worshipers and people who do obscene things. Men sleep with their fathers' wives and have intercourse with women who are menstruating.

All of the retributions for committing incest are evidences that God really abhor it and it's a sexual transgression and to avoid all of the embarrassments is to avoid the incest and that being an evidence and a benefit of sexual moderation.

AVOIDING HOMOSEXUALITY = Lev 18:22 ~

You shall not lie with a male as with a woman; it is an abomination.

Lev 20:13 ~

If a man lies with a male as with a woman, both of them have committed an abomination; they shall surely be put to death; their blood is upon them.

God requires the avoidance of gay sex and decrees death penalty to those who commit it just as he does with incest. The death was physical and instantaneous in the old testament but it's more of spiritual and slower in this new testament of the church.

Jude 1:7 ~

Just as Sodom and Gomorrah and the surrounding cities, which likewise indulged in sexual immorality and pursued unnatural desire, serve as an example by undergoing a punishment of eternal fire.

Using the old sodomites and Gomorraites as examples saint Jude warns Christians to shun gay and lesbian sexual activities, considering the eternal demnation and death they incur to their practitioners.

Rom 1:26-28

For this reason God gave them up to dishonourable passions. For their women exchanged natural relations for those that are contrary to nature; and the men likewise gave up natural relations with women and were consumed with passion for one another, men committing shameless acts with men and receiving in themselves the due penalty for their error. And since they did not see fit to acknowledge God, God gave them up to a debased mind to do what ought not to be done.

Apostle Paul encountered gross lesbianism and gay activities in Rome then he began to warn that the homosexual should stop it, only for him to discover they had sold their souls to the devil so that they couldn't think about repenting from it.

Gen 2:24 =

Therefore a man shall leave his father and his mother and hold fast to his wife, and they shall become one flesh.

Mark 10:6-9 ~

But from the beginning of creation, 'God made them male and female.' 'Therefore a man shall leave his father and mother and hold fast to his wife, and the two shall become one flesh.' So they are no longer two but one flesh. What therefore God has joined together, let not man separate."

We are reminded of monogamy which is the only sexual life God constituted and endorses, And there should be no contradiction to it.

1ˢᵗ Cor 6:9-10 –

Or do you not know that the unrighteous will not inherit the kingdom of God? Do not be deceived: neither the sexually immoral, nor idolaters, nor adulterers, nor men who practice homosexuality, nor thieves, nor the greedy, nor drunkards, nor revilers, nor swindlers will inherit the kingdom of God.

1ˢᵗ Tim 1:8-11 ESV –

Now we know that the law is good, if one uses it lawfully, understanding this, that the law is not laid down for the just but for the lawless and disobedient, for the ungodly and sinners, for the unholy and profane, for those who strike their fathers and mothers, for murderers, the sexually immoral, men who practice homosexuality, enslavers, liars, perjurers, and whatever else is contrary to sound doctrine, in accordance with the gospel of the glory of the blessed God with which I have been entrusted.

1ˢᵗ Cor 7:2 –

But because of the temptation to sexual immorality, each man should have his own wife and each woman her own husband.

2ⁿᵈ Cor 5:17 –

Therefore, if anyone is in Christ, he is a new creation. The old has passed away; behold, the new has come.

1ˢᵗ Cor 6:9-11

9 Or do you not know that wrongdoers will not inherit the kingdom of God? Do not be deceived: Neither the sexually immoral nor idolaters nor adulterers nor men who have sex with men 10 nor thieves nor the greedy nor drunkards nor slanderers nor swindlers will inherit the kingdom of God. 11 And that is what some of you were. But you were washed, you were sanctified, you were justified in the name of the Lord Jesus Christ and by the Spirit of our God.

1st Tim 1:8-11

8 We know that the law is good if one uses it properly. 9 We also know that the law is made not for the righteous but for lawbreakers and rebels, the ungodly and sinful, the unholy and irreligious, for those who kill their fathers or mothers, for murderers, 10 for the sexually immoral, for those practicing homosexuality, for slave traders and liars and perjurers—and for whatever else is contrary to the sound doctrine. 11 that conforms to the gospel concerning the glory of the blessed God, which he entrusted to me.

Apostle Paul continues to warn the whole churches and humanity all over the world to desist from homosexuality and all other kinds of sexual immorality, pointing to it's pollution of the church and its contagiousness to others, including the eternal doom it poses to sexual immorals, establishing the fact that refraining from sexual immorality is the key to be free from the dooms and to be at peace with God by sexual moderation.

All sorts of sexual immorality are ruinous but moderate sex life by monogamy is edifying in the individuals and universal church and althrough humans societies.

Chapter 5

MODERATING RELATIONSHIPS.

DEFINITION = Threading with caution while associating with people for any reason.

MEMORY VERSE = *Prov 13:20 ESV =*

Whoever walks with the wise becomes wise, but the companion of fools will suffer harm.

INTRODUCTION

People can be righteous in some ways, and still fall victims of unrighteousness in one or more other ways, relationship is one of the meanses through which people can execute righteousness or dwell In sin. So people should bear the responsibility of being diligent concerning the kinds of relationships they get involved and being diligent in choosing the kinds of people to relate with, so to not be drawn into sinful acts which emanate from ungodly and unwise relations, but the people of concern choosing the right people, who delight in godliness and wisdom and all legal episodes of life, whom they should relate with, so to walk and remain in the path of righteousness by relationships and to prevent themselves from the dangers of unrighteousness and foolishness.

---

i = RESTRAINING FROM BARBARIANS = (Prov 1:10-19 ESV).

[10] My son, if sinners entice you, do not consent. [11] If they say, "Come with us, let us lie in wait for blood; let us ambush the innocent without reason; [12] like Sheol let us swallow them alive, and whole, like those who go down to the pit; [13] we shall find all precious goods, we shall fill our houses with plunder; [14] throw in your lot among us; we will all have one purse"— [15] my son, do not walk in the way with them; hold back your foot from their paths, [16] for their feet run to evil, and they make haste to shed blood. [17] For in vain is a net spread in the sight of any bird, [18] but these men lie in wait for their own blood; they set an ambush for their own lives. [19] Such are the ways of everyone who is greedy for unjust gain; it takes away the life of its possessors.

SUPPORTING TEXTS = Ps 1:1; Eph 5:11.

Barbarians are group of people who venture in assaulting others, Wounding or killing them and eventually rob them of their resources, all the acts of the barbarians being evil; God forbids barbarity and wills that it should be forbidden by all who desire living a life of contentment to righteousness. And forbidden barbarity should be accomplished by refraining wholly from its perpetrators, hence righteousness by shunning barbarians and barbarity is evident and divinely endorsed. And more benefit of shunning it is avoiding the damage you should contribute to others and there is no guarantee of the perpetrators living so long and not to lose their own lives and fortunes through it.

ii = RESTRAINING FROM WAYWARD FELLOWS = (Prov 2:10-22 ESV)

[10] for wisdom will come into your heart, and knowledge will be pleasant to your soul; [11] discretion will watch over you, understanding will guard you, [12] delivering you from the way of evil, from men of perverted speech, [13] who forsake the paths of uprightness to walk in the ways of darkness, [14] who rejoice in doing evil and delight in the perverseness of evil, [15] men whose paths are crooked, and who are devious in their ways. [16] So you will be delivered from the forbidden woman, from the adulteress with her smooth words, [17] who forsakes the companion of her youth and forgets the covenant of her God; [18] for her house sinks down to death, and her paths to the departed; [19] none who go to her come back, nor do they regain the paths of life. [20] So you will walk in the way of the good and keep to the paths of the righteous. [21] For the upright will inhabit the land, and those with integrity will remain in it, [22] but the wicked will be cut off from the land, and the treacherous will be rooted out of it.

It is good and righteous to restrain from those who are persistently wayward almost in all their dealings. Wayward can sometimes be displayed due to difficulties, but it is developed to character when it is untamed by its exhibitors. Preaching of repentance changes the remorseful repentant from wayward attitudes, but the reprobates stick to it and never repent. However; the wise are to repent from waywardness, if they are still living therein, and they should absolutely shun their wayward acquaintances, who symbolically stand as thorns of waywardness in the flesh of the expectants of righteous living by relationship. Association is very influential either positively or negatively so intimating with epicurean and frivolous people have the influence of sensuality but intimating with godly and wise adventuring people have the influence of righteousness and good productivity.

iii = RESTRAINING FROM VILLAINS = (Prv 3:31-33, KJV).

Strive not with a man without cause if he had done thee No harm. V 31. Envy thou not the oppressor, and choose non of his ways. V 32. For the forward is abomination to the lord: but his secret is with the righteous. V 32 . (Prv 24:1-2, KJV) = Be thou not envious against evil men, Neither desire to be with them. V 1. = For their heart studieth destruction, and their lips talk of mischief. V 2 .

SUPPORTING TEXTS = Ps 37:1; 73:3.

Here is counsel, warning and exhortation to refrain from both, villainousness and the villains. This is because, villainousness is a sin of perversity, while taking part in it, is a way of promoting the same. Therefore righteousness by relationships demands total refrain from villainesses, villains and to concentrate on living social legal life which is a part of righteousness, furthermore living the godly principled life in accordance with God's laws from the bible. The villains are in most cases not barbaric but are stupid trouble makers. And they always influence anyone who intimates with them to becoming like them. Those who fall and are trapped by them are those who have initially chosen to be like them and those of their unwilling victims who cannot decide for themselves to breakout in a revolution to free themselves, and they get stuck therefore in the company of the villains and villainesses. The best thing to do is to never desire villainousness and to prevent self from the troublous consequences it genders.

iv = RESTRAINING FROM SEXUAL IMMORALS =
(Prv 5:3-8, KJV).

For the lips of a strange woman drops as an honeycomb, and her mouth is smoother than oil. V 3. But her end is bitter as wormwood, sharp as a two edged sword. V 4 . Her feet go down to death; her steps take hold on hell. V 5 . Lest thou should ponder the path of life, her ways are movable, that thou canst not know them . V 6 . How me now therefore, o ye children, and depart not from the words of my mouth. V 7 . Remove thy way far from her, and come not nigh the door of her house . V 8

SUPPORTING TEXTS = Prv 2:16-20; Prv 6:23-26; Prv chapter 7; Prv 9:13-18 ; Ezek 20:30;Rom 16:17; Col 2:8-10; 1 Thes 5:19-22; 2 Pet 2:14-17 .

The anonymous Potiphar's wife is one of the biblical examples of loose women who delight in enticing and seducing young and aged men sexually. As it is known that immoral sex is a sin and having it with other men's wives is worse. Whether men are enticed by the loose women or otherwise; It's the duty of both men and women who are enticed to discipline themselves and restrain from their enticers and from the sex contents of their enticement, without which expressing righteousness by relationships is interrupted and it sabotages many other aspects of principles of righteous living by relating to others, both male and female. The book of proverbs chapter 6, records a skilfully seductive woman who lure those who desire her into having sexual immorality with her , and she leading them into destroying their future, destinies and lives. However the diligent consider the consequences of having intimacy with the sexual immorals and they try to discipline their desires to relating with them.

> v = **DESPISING AND RESTRAINING FROM FOOLS** =
>   **(Prv 13:20, KJV).**

> *He that walketh with wise men shall be wise: But a companion of fools shall be destroyed.*

> = *(Isah 32:6 AMPC)* =

> *For the fool speaks folly and his mind plans iniquity: practicing profane ungodliness and speaking error concerning the Lord, leaving the craving of the hungry unsatisfied and causing the drink of the thirsty to fail.*

The fear of God is the starting point of wisdom exhibited by those who have reverential and worshipful fear of God. And sinning is the asymmetrical outcome of foolishness of all sorts. Being informed about this, it makes sense to be careful in our dealings pertaining the fools with their foolishness, and dealing with and conquering sin producing foolishness is unachievable if the fools themselves are not conquered through refraining from their sins. fools are negatively Influential to their acquaintances in the sense that they lure them into slandering God, godliness and the godly with them. The acquaintances of the fools have the tasks of avoiding the fools so not to be drawn and dwell into sinning through foolish acts with the proper fools. The diligent who can appreciate this information are to quench their desires to mingling with the anti God critical fool. Every persistent sinner is a fool.

vi = SEPARATING FROM THE ILLTEMPERED = (Prv 22:24-25, AMP).

Make no friendships with a man given to anger, and with a wrathful man do mot associate. V 24. Lest you learn his ways and get yourself into a snare. V 25.

Anger can be right when it is intended to correct things and promote righteousness. But excess of anger is a sin, also hoarding and expressing untamed anger as an attitude is the more a disaster. Therefore each individual should endeavour to moderate his or her anger, applying anger for augmenting matters rather than worsening things by uncontrolled anger. Though we are to be offended by others against our gentle lives and will, yet we are to be self disciplined enough to moderate our anger by disciplining our temper from where the anger manifest into the outwards. We are also to restrain from fellows whom we have discerned to be unable to tame their temper but are subject to the rules of ill temper, because a continual companying with such a people attracts evil and sinful influence of learning and living in like manner of hot temper exhibition like them, and thereby dwell in sin and victimisation of immoderate anger. Some people brag with their attitude of getting furiously and disastrously angry at some points and some other people wish to become like them in that kind of attitude. But the wisdom of the prudent ceases them from desiring to be careless associate of the imprudent and chronic wrathful fellows. And by doing this, the prudent exempt themselves from participating in the foolish and sinful anger.

*vii = **APPLYING GODLY WISDOM** = (Prv 29:3, KJV).*

Whoso loveth wisdom rejoiceth his father: but he that keepeth company with harlots spendeth his substance.

Applying Godly wisdom and shunning self conceit and self justification, in relating with people is a means of moderating relationships. It is therefore necessary that, Godly wisdom should not be ignored in relating with people as it is one of the principles to executing righteousness through relationships. The godly wisdom gives the proper revelation of the results of every desired and intended adventure to prepare the godly wise in favour of good adventure and against bad adventures. Then the wise stands the chance of making the right decision, talking the right step to engaging in the good ventures of which good relationship is one and to shun evil ventures exemplified by bad relationship.

*viii = **MINIMISING NEIGHBOURLY VISITING** = (Prv 27:17, NAS).*

Let your foot rarely be in your neighbour's house, or he will become weary of you and hate you.

Visiting can be excessive and sinful, hence people should be diligent and moderate in visiting others no matter how dearly the supposed visited people may be to the visitors. If visiting is not moderated the supposed visited people will certainly be saddened by over visitation from their visitors to them. In some occasions, searching for fun, proving personal love for, or profiteering venturing can be some of the reasons of visiting people, though the mentioned reasons can be genuine, the visitors must not abuse themselves to their supposed visited acquaintances, so not to be seeing as being worrisome to the supposed visited ones. And sometimes the visited acquaintances, will misunderstand, misinterpret, and wrongly respond to the visitors believing that the visitors constantly visit them for the self interests of the visitors. And in some other occasions the visitors excessively visit their acquaintances treacherously hunting to attain their self interest through their regular visits to their acquaintances. Excess visitation results in the visitors losing their respect to the visited. So the desires to be visiting people too often more than they can accept must be quenched by the visitors.

MODERATING ZEAL

DEFINITION = 1 = Being very effective to doing things with diligence.

2 = The ability to control the eagerness to get things done.

3 = Applying zeal to right purposes.

MEMORY VERSES = *Phil 3:13-14 AMPC =*

> *[13] I do not consider, brethren, that I have captured and made it my own [yet]; but one thing I do [it is my one aspiration]: forgetting what lies behind and straining forward to what lies ahead, [14] I press on toward the goal to win the [supreme and heavenly] prize to which God in Christ Jesus is calling us upward.*

INTRODUCTION

The majority of us humans are so zealous with doing one thing or another. Each person is zealous in his or her own areas of pursuit. Everyone has his or her ambitions whether for good or for bad and each of us wants his own or her own ambition/s to be achieved. Jesus Christ and the angels are zealous for advancing the kingdom of God in heaven and on earth but Satan and his co demons are zealous to sabotaging the kingdom of God from heaven to earth and to advance their own kingdom. Jesus and Christian soldiers of the cross are so zealous to achieving wellbeing of the church and entire humans but Satan and his human emissaries are so zealous to executing wickedness on humans all over the world. Some people among the social government and religious and church governments are zealous to governing the people well while some of them are so zealous to governing the people wrongly. Some Christians are serious for the church development while the majority are zealous to corrupting it. Likewise some religionists and socialists are zealot builders while the majority are zealous corrupters.

There are also people with rash zeal. This is the kind of people who are zealous to championing some things but being ignorant of the real purposes of what they are championing. The emphasis of this chapter of the book is to disclose the principles of engaging our zeal appropriately and to achieve good results.

---

i = TAKING PRECAUTION BEFORE ACTING =
(Prv 4:26-27,AMP)

Consider well the path of your feet, and let your ways be established and ordered aright. V 26. Turn not aside to the right hand or to the left; remove your foot from evil. V 27.

= (Prov 14:16, AMPC) =

A wise man suspects danger and cautiously avoids evil, but the fool bears himself insolently and is [presumptuously] confident.

SUPPORTING TEXT = Ps 1:1; Eph 5:11.

We are to be diligent concerning our dealings, and ensure we don't invest our time, energy and resources on patronising evils and dangerous mistakes. Rather our energy, time and zeal should be invested in righteous activities, as it is understood that, by doing so, our zeal is moderated. There are at times daftness stupefy some people that they choose to engage into some actions and adventures while they're unable to realise the repercussions of those adventures and actions. Sometimes they may realise the repercussions yet they continue their move into them due to their ego which they want to protect through arrogance. But the prudent look very well before they leap. They never permit their ego to takeover their choices, decisions and actions, so they carefully think, observe and have second thoughts, being prepared to stay back if there are repercussions awaiting for whoever that engages into their intended ventures and actions, and they're never being controlled by their compelling but unpurposed zeal and by so doing they prevent themselves from many avoidable troubles, including avoidable sins.

ii = DESPISING RASH ZEAL AND EXERCISING GODLY PATIENCE = (Prv 19:2, AMP).

Desire without knowledge is not good, and to be over hasty is to sin and miss the mark .

= (Prv 21:5, AMP) =

The thoughts of the(steadily) diligent tend only to plenteousness But everyone who is impatient and hasty hastens only to poverty.

= (Prv 25:8-10, AMP) =

*Rush not soon to quarrel(before magistrate or elsewhere),
lest you know not what to do in the end, when your neighbours
have put you to shame. V 8 . Argue your cause with your
neighbour himself; discover not and disclose not another's
secret. V 9. Lest he who hears you revile you and bring shame
upon you and your ill repute will have no end. V 10 .*

The zestful must be diligent, and not reckless, in whatever
they are engaged or they're yet to engage to do. Rash zeal
attracts disappointment from, disputes, quarrelling, irrational
controversy and rash venturing. It is wise and right to ponder
upon the outcomes of venture, controversy, disputes and
quarrels whether we are right and will be innocent in the
end, before commencing them. It is a sin to quarrel, being
controversial, and venturing zealously in unrighteous manners.
But righteousness by moderating zeal can be achievable by,
ensuring that, the zeal for controversy, venturing, quarrelling is
applied for rightful self defense and promoting global godliness.
However: it is wiser to understand and live by the principle of
never strive to win every argument even when you're right with
your points and views. Even the bible warns the church through
apostle Paul to never struggle for winning every argument,
because it causes strife and spiritual pollution.

= (2nd Tim 2:15-18 AMPC) =

*[15] Study and be eager and do your utmost to present
yourself to God approved (tested by trial), a workman
who has no cause to be ashamed, correctly analyzing and
accurately dividing [rightly handling and skillfully teaching]
the Word of Truth. [16] But avoid all empty (vain, useless, idle)*

*talk, for it will lead people into more and more ungodliness.
[17] And their teaching [will devour; it] will eat its way like
cancer or spread like gangrene. So it is with Hymenaeus and
Philetus, [18] Who have missed the mark and swerved from
the truth by arguing that the resurrection has already taken
place. They are undermining the faith of some.*

Beside protecting the integrity of Christian teaching are there
many other events which challenge our patience and many
people falling for them. The typical example is the majority of
us humans despising God's requirement of exercising patience
against anxiety.

= (Matt 6:33 AMPC) =

*[33] But seek (aim at and strive after) first of all His kingdom
and His righteousness (His way of doing and being right), and
then all these things taken together will be given you besides.*

Most people through their rash zeal begin to pursue other things
first and the kingdom of God in their lives and on earth second,
while some pursue only other things for themselves and forget
about the kingdom of God totally. But few are those who really live
with godly patience and overcome anxiety and rash zeal in many
ways and to as such God relates intimately giving them some super
revelations of his way and super opportunities for excellence.

*iii = SHUNNING SELF VENGEANCE, DEPENDING ON GOD'S
VENGEANCE =*

= (Prv 22:20,24, AMP) =

*Do not say, I will repay evil; wait(expectantly) for the Lord,
and he will rescue you. V 20 .*

Man's steps are ordered by the Lord, how then can a man understand his way? V 24 .

= (Prv 24:28-29, AMP) =

Be not a witness against your neighbour without cause, and deceive not with your lips. V 28. Say not, I will do to him the same way he has done to me: I will pay him back for his deed. V 29.

SUPPORTING TEXT = Matt 5:25,39,44; Matt 18:15; Rom 12:17,19; Eph 4:25.

We are dare to be offended by others in various ways, but we should always ponder upon the word of God, which says vengeance belongs to God . Therefore we are not to be sinning through self vengeance but we should moderate our vengeance by committing our cases to God and by faith expecting his vengeance upon our adversaries. And God will always avenge for us in his own ways, nonetheless; the most important matter here should be that, no sin should be committed through self vengeance and vengeance being moderate for allowing God to execute the righteous and perfect vengeance for the offended. Self vengeance is one other means some people express their ungodly impatience, though for real waiting for God to avenge for us is easy to be said but not easy to be done, yet doing it is the wisdom and basic factor for real victory. There are many other ways some people use their rash zeal to replace their patience with God and they swing into rash actions, only to be disappointed and regretting but not with the prudent with godly patience who quietly have success in every respect just by being self disciplined to be contented and patient in God, and God doing for them those good things which they cannot do for themselves.

iv = SHUNNING SENSUALITY = (Prov 31:2-7 NKJV).

[2] What, my son? And what, son of my womb? And what, son of my vows? [3] Do not give your strength to women, Nor your ways to that which destroys kings. [4] It is not for kings, O Lemuel, It is not for kings to drink wine, Nor for princes intoxicating drink; [5] Lest they drink and forget the law, And pervert the justice of all the afflicted. [6] Give strong drink to him who is perishing, And wine to those who are bitter of heart. [7] Let him drink and forget his poverty, And remember his misery no more.

Traditional kings and all other traditional together with political leaders are warned to be ethical with their zeal in regard to sensuality and diligence. They are hinted on the dangers of being zealous with sexual immorality and drunkenness which are losing dominion power and misjudging the people under alcoholic intoxication. They're also told that those who are zealous with these two kinds of life more of their likes are those who take their own future and destinies for granted, giving them these few exemplary reasons to moderate their zeal for appetites and consumption. We Christians are godly kings and priests who should model the moderation of zeal for consumption and to live a contented life with it and to avoid the troubles of zealously undisciplined consumption manner. Every human is required by God to moderate their zeal of consumption and to live in contentment in the area of consumption life.

v = SHUNNING PERSISTENT ROBBERY = (Deut 16:19 NKJV).

You shall not pervert justice; you shall not show partiality, nor take a bribe, for a bribe blinds the eyes of the wise and twists the words of the righteous.

= (1ˢᵗ Sam 8:1-3 NKJV) =

[1] Now it came to pass when Samuel was old that he made his sons judges over Israel. [2] The name of his firstborn was Joel, and the name of his second, Abijah; they were judges in Beersheba. [3] But his sons did not walk in his ways; they turned aside after dishonest gain, took bribes, and perverted justice.

SUPPORTING TEXTS = 2nd Chron 19:2; Ps 26:10; Prv 17:23; Isah 1:23; Isah 5:23; Isah 33:15;

The professional lawyers and judges who take bribe to pervert judgements are zealot thieves, some of the kings of the Israelites of the old who perverted judgements for taking bribes were typical examples of those with the zeal for robbery. All takers of bribes are zealous thieves and those who give them the bribes are the engineers of the thievery. They make their victims discontent in many ways and the discontentment rebound to them in different ways. We all are required to moderate our zeal to be contented with what we can get by being truthful and fair with judgement and every other human affairs. And to live contentedly with the positive results of our zealous uprightness.

vi = BEING A DILIGENT PROVIDER = (Prov 15:6 NKJV).

In the house of the righteous there is much treasure, But in the revenue of the wicked is trouble.

= (Prov 21:20 NKJV) =

There is desirable treasure, And oil in the dwelling of the wise, But a foolish man squanders it.

= (Prov 24:3-4 NKJV) =

[3] Through wisdom a house is built, And by understanding it is established; [4] By knowledge the rooms are filled With all precious and pleasant riches.

The matter of providing personal needs and the needs of others requires intensive work, and there is a vast difference between working hard and working smartly. There are people who work hard and smartly at the same time, there are those who do not work hard but work smartly while there are others who work hard but not working smartly. All of the works are aimed at production and provision but when purpose and priorities are misunderstood abuses are inevitable. Some people work, get the dividends of their works but squander them unnecessarily, while there are those who use the dividends of their works wisely. The focal point of this section is to call attention to the fact that working diligently and providing diligently is the key to moderating the zeal for provision and to have a life of contentment in the aspect of personal Providence in addition to God's Providence for each of us.

Chapter 7

MODERATING GIVING

DEFINITION = Giving willingly, comfortably and purposely.

MEMORY VERSE = *2 Cor 9:7 AMPC =*

> *[7] Let each one [give] as he has made up his own mind and purposed in his heart, not reluctantly or sorrowfully or under compulsion, for God loves (He takes pleasure in, prizes above other things, and is unwilling to abandon or to do without) a cheerful (joyous, "prompt to do it") giver [whose heart is in his giving]. [Prov. 22:9.]*

INTRODUCTION

Giving is a part of Life and it must not be ignored while dealing with people and our collective affairs. There are universal dimensions of giving and of things to give. Time can be give, attention can be given, emotion, service, energy, power, skills, education trust, love , hate, jealousy, envy, gratitude, ingratitude, bad and good advises can be given, money and other substances can also be given. All of the mentioned are not all that can be given from among all humans.

The subject matter is about giving them moderately. Most people are immoderate with their generous life, in the sense that they give with their selfish motives or under coarseness or under compulsion. The minority of humans are moderate givers who give willingly, prudently, comfortably and selflessly. God is the universal and greatest moderate giver who gives to all of his creatures selflessly and comfortably, even to the extent of giving his only son Jesus Christ for salvation of the sinful mankind, and Jesus giving his own life and true Christianity to the world. Satan and his collaborators are givers who don't giver good things but they give bad things. So anybody can be a giver, but what really matters is what the person gives. You're about to read on how to be disciplined in giving and of the advantages of doing it. Some people devastate the lives of others by immoderate giving, some people devastate their own lives by their own immoderate giving. But the moderate givers build the both of their own life and the lives of others.

---

i = SHUNNING PARSIMONY AND BEING LIBERAL TO GOD =
(Prv 3:9-10, KJV).

Honour the Lord with thy substance, and with the first fruit of thine increase. V 9. So shall thy barn be filled with plenty, and thy press shall burst out with new wine. V 10.

SUPPORTING TEXTS = Lev 19:13; Deut 24:15; Deut 28:8.

There is nothing wrong about giving to God, but giving to God doesn't encourage evil venturing to earn money and other things which should be given to him or God blessing illicit means of profiting just because the illicit adventurers are generous to him.

The giving to God must not be with grudging but according to personal capabilities with cheerfulness of the heart. Because God's service require money and other resources to be run, meanwhile God does not rain money to his servants from heaven, rather God blesses humans to bless his service, so we are to despise stinginess against God, his services and servants, yet we should endeavour to identify real God's servants and true church of God where our offerings, donations and tithes should be beneficial for welfare and progress of the church and circular entities. Poor sponsorship is a major cause of the slow progress of the church but good sponsorship gives it a speedy progress when it's lead by the holy spirit.

ii = BEING LIBERAL TO NEIGHBOURHOODS = (Prv 3:27-28, KJV).

Withhold not good from them to whom it is due, when bit is in the power of thine hand to do it. V 27. Say not to thy neighbour, go, and come again, and tomorrow I will give, when thou hast it by thee . V 28.

SUPPORTING TEXTS = Lev 19:13; Deut 24:15; Rom 13:7; Gal 6:10.

God blesses people to be leaders, rich and advantaged in different areas of life. The people's God given privilege can place them in the positions of possessing the rights, privileges of others and having personal capacities of helping others. The privileges, rights of others in the possessions of the leaders and other advantaged people should not be withheld and delayed in giving them to the rightful owners of the rights and privileges, considering that the leaders are placed to manage the rights and privileges of the people and manage them well. And the personal assistance the advantaged should render to others must be done promptly to help the needy and the owners of the rights and privileges taking advantages of what belong to or what is freely given to them at the needful moments. Releasing the rights and privileges to the rightful owners without sentiments and giving of alms to the needy at their times of need without delay or total denial through stinginess is expressing righteousness by moderately giving rights and privileges to fellow humans. It's also an expression of self discipline by selfless releasing of the rights and privileges of the people.

> **DESPISING PARSIMONY AND POSSESSING LIBERAL NATURE = (Prv 11:24-26, KJV).**
>
> **There is that scattereth yet increaseth; and there is that withholdeth more than is meet, but it tends to poverty. V 24. The liberal soul shall be made fat, and he that watereth shall be watered also himself . V 25. He that withholdeth corn, the people shall curse him: But blessing shall be upon the head of him that selleth it. V 26 .**
>
> **SUPPORTING TEXT = 2 Cor 9:6-10 .**

Possessing the nature of parsimony is a sin and being parsimonious is progressing in sin of selfishness and greed. But moderating stinginess requires, being naturally generous and expressing it by willing giving of alms to the needy not for ostentation, nor beyond personal ability but with philanthropic natural exhibition. Doing so is exhibiting righteousness and moderating giving by natural philanthropy.

*iii = **CONQUERING VENGEANCE WITH GENEROSITY** =*
(Prv 25:21-22, KJV).

If thine enemy be hungry, give him bread to eat; and if he be thirsty, give him water to drink . V 21. For thou shalt heap a coal of fire upon his head, and the Lord shall reward thee. V 22.

SUPPORTING TEXT = Matt 5:44; Rom 12:20 .

If we consider how we are being offended by others we should conclude that, our offenders don't deserve our alms and helps of all sorts. But the word of God guides us otherwise. God wills we should moderate giving of alms and other forms of hospitality by shunning self vengeance by stinginess and total deprivation against our offenders. And it is to be done by despising the offenses committed against us when it comes to the point of helping even those who do often offend and ridicule us, mostly when they are helpless and our helps to them can settle their cases. While having done so; we should depend on God for the reward of our righteousness, through shunning self vengeance and helping our antagonists by proffering financial, material, food and generic hospitality to them.

= (Prov 21:14 AMPC) =

A gift in secret pacifies and turns away anger, and a bribe in the lap, strong wrath.

In other ways: there are deceitful givers who give cunningly to those they have offended only to appease them and buy their conscience and consent for reconciliation. In another way the cunning giver use bribes to achieve the same goal. But the real show should be the offenders to give apology first to the offended, seconded by free will giving from the offenders to them after they have happily and genuinely reconciled with the offenders.

iv = GIVING TO THE NEEDY = (Prv 19:17, KJV)

He that hath pity upon the poor lendeth unto the Lord, And that which he hath given will he pay him again.

= (Prv 22:9, KJV) =

He that hath a bountiful eyes shall be blessed, for he giveth of his bread to the poor.

= (Prv 28:27, KJV) =

He that giveth unto the poor shall not lack, But he that hideth his eyes shall have many a curse.

= (Prv 31:20, KJV) =

She strecheth out her hand to the poor, Yea, she reacheth out her hands to the needy.

SUPPORTING TEXTS.

Deut 15:7; Eccl 11:1; Matt 10:42; Matt 25:40; 2 Cor 9:6-19; Heb 6:10 .

It's true that people in some ways give financial and service assistance to the needy, yet helping the needy is a divine obligation with divine rewards to those who bears the responsibility of willingly helping the them by finance, other material gifts and services. Curses is meted to those who choose to be excessively stingy to the needy and blessings for the philanthropists to the needy. Hence it is a righteousness to patronise the needy based one personal capacity. Shunning parsimony by being generous to the needy is exhibition of righteousness through giving. There is a different between people who intend to be helpful to the needy but do not have what to offer them, from those who comfortably have what to give to the needy but by wickedness refuse to give it out. Moderate giving to the poor and needy requires giving to them at the slightest comfortable moment.

There is the necessity to help people by giving of alms and services but the giving should not lead the giver into involving into illicit venturing so to meet his or her responsibility of giving. But the giver should give cheerfully both to God and to people from his or her legal incomes and services. Though there are more ways of giving both to God and man which are not listed in the lessons, the conclusion of the whole matter here is that righteousness and discipline by moderating giving, which is possible by shunning excess stinginess and be willingly, rightfully and cheerfully financially, materially and morally patriotic and other such generosity are obligatory in relating with and serving the Lord God.

To read and know in a more detail about giving: You should read my book titled **LIVING A GENEROUS LIFE** *(From points of reality).*

MODERATING THOUGHTS.

DEFINITION = Being conscious of what we think about and to eradicate the negative thoughts from our minds while accommodating the positive thoughts in them.

MEMORY VERSE = *Matt 12:34-35 KJV*

> *[34] O generation of vipers, how can ye, being evil, speak good things? For out of the abundance of the heart the mouth speaketh. [35] A good man out of the good treasure of the heart bringeth forth good things: and an evil man out of the evil treasure bringeth forth evil things.*
>
> *= (Prov 4:23 Amp) =*
>
> *[23] Keep and guard your heart with all vigilance and above all that you guard, for out of it flow the springs of life.*
>
> *= (Prov 23:7 AMPC) =*
>
> *[7] For as he thinks in his heart, so is he. As one who reckons, he says to you, eat and drink, yet his heart is not with you [but is grudging the cost].*

INTRODUCTION

It seems sins are external only, hence many people are unaware that sins can be committed internally, which is exemplified by impure and all rounds of negative and injurious thinking. Beside polluted and sinful thoughts are sinful emotions as exemplified by emotionally mental Immoral sex, envy and jealousy, while the said mental lustful sex, envy and jealousy erupt from selfish evil thought.

It is now quite comprehensible that, Sins are committed in various ways, so people are to be conscious of the kinds of thoughts they permit and harbour into their minds, so to not commit sin and continue to do so inside of the mind. For moderating thoughts, people are responsible for eliminating evil thoughts from their various hearts by, prayer, endeavouring to be self disciplined in the divine law of righteousness and consistently living in holiness, which is practicable only by embracing all righteous and positive devices, hoarding them in the minds and possessing and applying them as necessary hobbies. Righteousness is promoted by moderating thoughts, evident in conquering evil thoughts with good thoughts.

> *i = RATIONALISING ABOUT PERSONAL ACTIONS =*
> *(Prv 4:23,26, NAS)*

> *Watch over your heart with all diligence, for from it flows the springs of life. V 23 . Watch the path of your feet and all your ways will be Established. V 26.*

We are divinely mandated to be extremely careful in managing our hearts, because the heart is the initial natural vessel from which all external behaviours and words are prompted, both good and evil behaviours and words are products of the mindsets. And we are to despise all sorts of evil words and behaviours while promoting the good ones in our lives. But it's unachievable without conquering negative thoughts and clinging to positive thoughts.

ii = CONQUERING PERVERSE THOUGHTS WITH UPRIGHT THINKING = (Prov 12:5, 20 AMPC)

[5] The thoughts and purposes of the [consistently] righteous are honest and reliable, but the counsels and designs of the wicked are treacherous. [20] Deceit is in the hearts of those who devise evil, but for the counselors of peace there is joy.

= (Prv 15:26, KJV) =

The thoughts of the wicked are abomination to the lord: but the words of the pure are pleasant words .

Good thoughts and good words are pleasing to God, while he is displeased with evil thoughts and evil words. There are different ways of speaking both the good and evil words, which are known to be products of the mindsets. Good or evil counselling are two ways of speaking good or evil as the texts have them.

Then we have our personal responsibility of eliminating all selfishness generated evil thoughts which evil counselling portrays, then we are to esteem selfless thoughts and the selfless counselling they generate, and thus express righteousness by moderating thoughts as shown is eliminating evil counsels and giving good counselling to people. Sex perversion is a product of perverse thought over sex. Drug abuse is a result of abusive thoughts over taking of drugs. Injustice is a manifestation of unjust thoughts. But legal sex as in monogamy, legal consumption of drugs for cure, fair treatments and fair judgements are products of upright and moderate thoughts.

iii = DESPISING DISCOURAGING THOUGHTS, FOCUSING ON GODLY FAITH =

= (Prov 14:14, AMPC) =

The backslider in heart [from God and from fearing God] shall be filled with [the fruit of] his own ways, and a good man shall be satisfied with [the fruit of] his ways [with the holy thoughts and actions which his heart prompts and in which he delights].

= (Prv 16:3, AMP) =

Roll your works upon the lord (commit and trust them wholly to him; he will cause your thoughts to become agreeable to his will, and) so shall your plans be established and succeed.

Discouraging thoughts against God and his will rise in the heart sometimes as doubts about if God can grant victory to the Christians during their Christian trials times. Sometimes the discouraging ideas come as enticement from power of the flesh, other word human nature, the world or Satan himself, and in some occasions anti Godliness discouraging thoughts rise from devaluation of Pleasures of true godliness and esteeming deceitful pleasures of sin in life. However, divine law of moderation demands that the thoughts of the heart must be for prompting true godliness, doing the proper will of God, all to God's honour and glory and for personal benefit of the moderate thinker; Meanwhile doubts and lustful thoughts which attract discouragement in the Lord must be overcome with persistent godly faith and true self denial from the snares of enticements and carnal pleasures. Hence the thoughts are moderated by faith towards God and acceptance of life of contentment in the Lord, by which thoughts of discouragement against being in the Lord disappear from the heart: and righteousness by moderate thinking is exhibited.

iv = RELYING ON DIVINE INSPIRATION = (Prv 16:1-3, AMP)

The plans of the mind and orderly thinking belong to man, but from the Lord comes the (wise) answer of the tongue. V 1. All the ways of a man are pure In his own eyes, but the Lord weighs the spirit(the thoughts and intents of the heart). V 2. Roll your works upon the lord(commit and trust them wholly to him; he will cause your thoughts to become agreeable to his will) and so shall your plans be established and succeed. V 3.

= (Prv 20:24, KJV) =

Man's ways are ordered by the Lord, how can a man then understand his ways.

SUPPORTING TEXTS = 1st Sam 16:7; Heb 4:12.

Without divine inspiration we humans will always base our plans and responses to all questions pertaining to life on our humans philosophy, self righteousness and self justification. But with God Inspired thoughts in the minds of humans their plans are excellently accomplished and answers to all questions as life demands are perfectly provided by those whose thoughts God inspires. Refraining from mere humans philosophy and adapting to God's inspiration for proper thinking alludes righteousness by moderate thinking, and by moderate thinking plans are also moderated. Also by avoiding causes of failure through humans imperfections and employing God's directions for success, we can attain excellence of fulfillment.

v = SHUNNING ANXIETY, THINKING DILIGENTLY =
(Prov 21:5 AMPC).

The thoughts of the [steadily] diligent tend only to plenteousness, but everyone who is impatient and hasty hastens only to want.

Anxiety is as powerful as distracting people from thinking the right ways and thereby fall victims to prejudice and vague conclusions about their dealing with God, people, their personal endeavours and rightround life's affections, committing diverse offenses against humanity and sin against God. Also anxiety Is the force behind ungodly impatience, which causes most of both the Christians and non Christians to rush into many wrongly timed and reckless venturing and at times the impatient are driven away from God's plans and purposes concerning them. But righteousness is required by the way of moderating thinking while exercising patience. Then the planers and venturers would be psychologically settled to have fore knowledge of the outcomes to what they're to engage into before investing their intelligence, services, energy, vigour, time and material resources; and that means execution of righteousness by being truly patient, thinking moderately and venturing properly.

Further research will definitely proffer other areas of life and humans affairs in which proper and moderate reasoning is a prerequisite. It is therefore necessary that the exemplary lessons above pertaining to righteous thinking should be consistently pondered upon and using them as guiding tutoring to progressing in the observation of divine law of righteousness by moderate thinking.

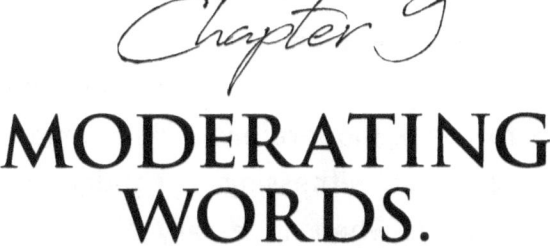

MODERATING WORDS.

DEFINITION = Talking with carefulness to avoid committing sin with what we say.

MEMORY VERSE = *Prov 25:11, AMPC*

> *A word fitly spoken and in due season is like apples of gold in settings of silver. [Prov. 15:23; Isa. 50:4.].*

INTRODUCTION

Words of the mouth can be utilised or abused in different ways. Some people are careless talkatives who use abusive words on their fellows without caring about the harms those words cause to the abused. Some of the careless talkatives use abusive words when they're provoked to anger or when they feel they're offended in any way, so they use the abusive words as their weapons of retaliation, disregarding the negative effects of their hostile comments either through ignorance or as a deliberate act. Some of the abusive talkatives do it as a result of bad habits they have developed in themselves over the years. As such intentionally talk down on others to intimidate and ridicule them, and to influence them and some other people with their sense of superiority to those they ridicule. False witnessing, unfair judgement, routine lies, bad advises, cursing unreasonably, and all other negative words are expression of verbal immoderation. This chapter has to disclose how to speak moderately, giving some examples of which some are = true witnessing, fair judgement, blessing, minimising our words when necessary, talking cautiously to avoid hurting other by what we say.

---

i = MINIMISING WORDS RATHER THAN TALKING STUPIDLY = (Prv 10:14,19, KJV).

Wise men store up knowledge (in mind and heart) but the mouth of the foolish is a present destruction. V 14. In a multitude of words transgression is not lacking, but he who restrains his lips is wise. V 19.

= (Prv 12:23, AMP) =

A prudent man is reluctant to display his knowledge, but the heart of (self confident) fools proclaims their folly.

= (Prv 13:3, AMP) =

He who guards his mouth keeps his life, but he who open wide his mouth comes to ruin.

= (Prv 29:11,20, AMP) =

A (self confident) fool utters all his anger, but a wise man holds it back and still. V 11. Do you see a man who is hasty in his words? There is more hope for (a self confident fool than for him. V 20.

= (Isah 32:6 AMPC) =

For the fool speaks folly and his mind plans iniquity: practicing profane ungodliness and speaking error concerning the Lord, leaving the craving of the hungry unsatisfied and causing the drink of the thirsty to fail.

In most cases people stupefy themselves and commit sins by being eager to talk when they don't really know what they should say and what they shouldn't say. Other sets of people by wisdom prefer keeping quiet than talking trash and commit sins thereby, and to talk wisely when the need calls for it.

Rather than talking senselessly through ignorance and ego through which the reckless talkers fool themselves before humans and commit sins against God. It is better for the ignorant to keep calm and in most occasions listen to learn while others mostly the knowledgeable speak than the ignorant sinning and abase themselves through hasty talks emanating from their pride and ego. Emulating the wise who refrain from hasty commenting rather than being hasty to talk and to end up talking stupidly and sinfully; is one of the mediums of displaying righteousness by words moderation.

ii = SHUNNING STUPID COMMENTS AND TALKING PRUDENTLY

= (Prv 14:3, AMP) =

In the fool's own mouth is the rod(to shame) his pride, but the wise men's lips preserve them.

= (Prv 15:2,28, AMP) =

The tongue of the wise utters knowledge rightly, but the mouth of the (self confident) fool pours out folly. V 2. The mind of the (uncompromisingly) righteous studies how to answer, but the mouth of the wicked pours out evil things. V 28 .

= (Prv 18:20-21, AMP) =

A man's (moral)self shall be filled with the fruit of his mouth; and with the consequences of his words (whether good or evil). V 20 Deal and life are in the power of the tongue, and those who indulge in it shall eat the fruit of it. V 21 .

= (Prv 25:11, AMP) =

There is gold and a multitude of pearl, but the lips of knowledge are a vase of preciousness(the most precious of all).

= (Prv 26:4-5, AMP) =

Answer not(a self confident) fool according to his folly, lest you also be like him. V 4 . Answer a (self confident) fool according to his folks, lest he be wise in his eyes and conceit. V 5.

= (Prv 31:26, AMP) =

She opens her mouth in skilful and godly wisdom, and on her tongue is the law of kindness(giving counsel and instruction).

= (Prv 15:4, Amp) =

A gentle tongue(with its healing power) is a tree of life, but wilful contrariness in it breaks down the spirit.

SUPPORTING TEXT = Job 28:12,16-19; Isa 32:6; Isa 50:4; Matt 12:37; Matt 16:1-4; Matt 21:24-27; 1st Pet 3:15.

Moderating words is one of the evidences of progressing in self discipline and maturity. Ironically; reckless and foolish talking discloses some branches of immaturity, which are emotional, intellectual and spiritual immaturity. The three listed aspects of life are vital to determining righteousness or sin as pertaining to all humans. It is therefore necessarily wise that men {humans} should control their: emotions, intellectual and spiritual life which are easily polluted through carelessness, carnally stupid comments being the examples of the pollutants of the said components of life. Hence we are obliged to be consistently mindful of what we say by first of all rationalising the effects of what we intend to say at all times whether they make senses and are right to humans affairs or they make no senses and are wrong and sinful to we the Sayers before we state them or not. Righteousness by moderation of words is evident in refraining from foolish and sinful talking, and to replace it with talking diligently. We are to be intentional to talking with prudence and to shun all sorts of imprudent comments.

iii = *DESTROYING IDLE TALKS WITH DILIGENT ACTIONS =*
   (Prv 14:23, AMP).

In all labour there is profit, but idle talks leads only to poverty.

= (Prov 22:13, AMPC) =

The sluggard says, There is a lion outside! I shall be slain in the streets.

= (Jms 2:12, 14 AMPC) =

[12] So speak and so act as [people should] who are to be judged under the law of liberty [the moral instruction given by Christ, especially about love]. [14] What is the use (profit), my brethren, for anyone to profess to have faith if he has no [good] works [to show for it]? Can [such] faith save [his soul]?

Truly unbeneficial talking and reluctance towards personal tasks lead to committing sin of idleness, laziness and empty talks, topped by unproductivity. But to execute righteousness by words moderation in this aspect, there is the need to talk less and diligently, accompanying the diligent talking with legal labours instead of confessing ambitions, boasting about ambitions, commending and verbally resenting the ventures and achievements of others, and neglecting personal legal duties which should lay the foundation for righteous prosperity and success. One good action is better than one thousand inactions, and one imperfect action is better than one thousand perfect words and perfect inactions. Some Christians are only Christians by the words of their mouths not by their acts {lifestyle}. So are some religionists. There are lots of socialists who declare much of their dreams but do Very little or never do anything at all to fulfilling those dreams. So any word that is not accompanied by actions of Whoever says it is an immoderate word, but speaking the proper words and swinging into proper actions to accomplish the purpose of the word is a moderate word. This is one of the reasons God says his spoken words don't return to him void (unproductive, unaccomplished). Talking and doing make effectiveness, while talking about the right things and doing them make wisdom of moderation.

iv = DEFEATING VERBAL ARROGANCE WITH TEACHABILITY = (Prv 15:14).

The mind of him who has understanding seeks knowledge and inquires after and crave it, but the mouth of the (self confident) feeds on folly.

(Isah 32:6 AMPC)

For the fool speaks folly and his mind plans iniquity: practicing profane ungodliness and speaking error concerning the Lord, leaving the craving of the hungry unsatisfied and causing the drink of the thirsty to fail.

Most people are naive and unteachable, evidenced by their verbal defence and obstinacy concerning some matters and never love learning for their amendments to correcting their errors. The otherwise (the teachable) kind of people prefer learning to improve their lives and attitudes, because they are humble to their correctors and receptive to corrections. This highlights on the fact that rarely anybody is perfect in knowledge, words and actions, but arrogance by being resistant to learning the right things while settling in errors and mediocrity in contrast to embracing corrections make the difference between the oral scoffers and the prudent teachable.

In the case of moderating words in this area teachability is the required wisdom for replacing proud and arrogantly oral self defense, self righteousness and self justification. Because verbal arrogance is a proof of sinning through wording, while exhibiting righteousness by moderating wording is to refrain from proudly arrogant nagging and being receptive to corrections and constantly being apt to learning.

(Prov 12:15 AMPC)

The way of a fool is right in his own eyes, but he who listens to counsel is wise. [Prov. 3:7; 9:9; 21:2] .

(Prov 18:2, ESV)

[2] A fool takes no pleasure in understanding, But only in expressing his opinion.

Being conceited and opinionated is another way the fools display their immoderate comments and arrogance. But the wise are rational and adaptive to superior reasons and opinions of others and they moderate their own opinions in this way.

v = REFUTING IGNORANCE BY PRUDENT TALKING =
(Prv 10:21, AMP).

The lips of the (uncompromisingly) righteous feed and guide many, but fools die for want of understanding and heart.

= (Prv 15:7,AMP) =

The lips of the wise disperse knowledge (sifting it as chaff from the grain) ; not so with minds and hearts of the self confident and foolish.

As ignorance is not an excuse in the civil law courts so it is with divine law court. Nobody will be acquitted from his/her sin by God, just because the sinner does so by ignorance. This is quite comprehensive as we know we are obliged to acquire the knowledge of sins and of righteousness through the contents of laws of God from his word. The knowledgeable are skilled in proclaiming the accurate insights they have both in circular education and in God's word and law of righteousness. On the contrary: the ignorant are perplexed to saying and doing the right things as God and man require. Also the ignorant are apt to erring for not knowing the right things to say and do, and thus keep offending many and sinning against God by their words and actions. However we are expected to do righteousness by word moderation and that cannot be attainable if there is lacking of the accurate comprehension of law of righteousness, and law of word moderation precisely as this case is. Rather to keep on erring orally through ignorance, there is the demand to defeat reluctance and arrogance to acquire God given knowledge of righteousness which is to guide the mind and tongue to reasoning properly and comment properly, whereas the right reasons and comments are to be complemented by right actions, then ignorance totally defeated.

ERADICATING HOSTILE COMMENTING BY COMMENTING KINDLY = (Prv 10:10-11, NAS).

He who winks the eye causes trouble, and a babbling fool will be ruined. V 10.

The mouth of a righteous man is a well of life, but the mouth of the wicked conceals violence.

= (Prv 13:2, NAS) =

From the fruit of a man's mouth he enjoys good, but the desire of the treacherous is violence.

= (Prv 15:1, NAS) =

A gentle answer turns away wrath, but a harsh word stirs up anger

= (Prv 16:13-14, NAS) =

Righteous lips are delight of kings, and he who speaks right is loved. V 13. The fury of a king is like messengers of death, but a wise man will pacify it. 14

= (Prv 25:15, NAS) =

By forbearance a ruler may be persuaded, and a soft tongue breaks the bone.

SUPPORTING TEXT = Gen 32:4; 1st Sam 25:24.

People do offend people and commit sins against God through violent speeches. While at time people display righteousness through kind speeches, but God wills we should totally conquer violent utterances of all sorts and replace them with incessant kind words to peoples of different ethnicities, nations, tribes and clans. We are also to do the same towards God the sovereign king and Lord, hence we are free from God's wrath and those of humans leaders and other fellows. Rather than being rude in words we are to humble ourselves and the self humility is to be obvious in our kind words with which we approach people and such kind words which we use on others even in their absence. God created everything he has created beside human being by his kind, wise and creative word. He is in the business of creating good situations to his faithful and in some limits to the sinners with the powers of hi kind word. We humans that God created in his similar aptitudes are to be kind and creative and developing with our words rather than being destructive with it. We must moderate what we say, so our words should be some contributing factors to bettering the life of humanity and our own life. We should not be instrumental to destroying people with our hostile comments.

*vi = **KEEPING PERSONAL AND PEOPLE'S CONFIDENTIAL MATTERS = (Prv 11:13, KJV).***

A tale bearer revealeth secrets: but he that is of a faithful spirit concealeth the matter.

= (Prv 20:19, KJV) =

He that goeth about as a tale bearer revealeth secrets: Therefore meddle not with him that flattereth with his lips.

(Prv 13:3, KJV) = He that keepeth his mouth keepeth his life, But he that openeth wide his lips shall have destruction.

SUPPORTING TEXT = Rom 16:16-17.

Sin in some cases is committed through verbosity which leads to talking foolishly and carelessly revealing both personal privacy and those of others. Oral sins are also committed through eagerness to telling stories about self and about others. Oral sin is also committed through gossiping. But whichever way, the law of righteousness by utterances demands that there should be moderation in speaking and that requires being diligent and rational prior to voicing whatever; so the sins of careless revelations of secrecy will be avoided and be replaced with silence when necessary and talking with prudence at the right times and in the right manner. Therefore it is wise to observe law of righteousness by orations through minimising words, talking prudently and keeping appropriate personal and other people's private matters as privates.

vii = DEMOTING FALSE WITNESSING BY TRUE WITNESSING = (Prv 12:17, AMP).

He who breaths out truth shows forth righteousness (uprightness and right standing with God). But a false witness utters deceit.

= (Prv 14:5,25, AMP) =

A faithful witness shall not lie, but a false witness breaths out falsehood. V 5. A truthful witness saves life, but a deceitful witness speaks lies (and endanger lives). V 25.

= (Prv 21:28, AMP) =

A false witness will perish, but the word of a man who hears attentively will endure and go unchallenged.

= (Prv 24:28-29, AMP) =

Be not a witness against your neighbour without cause, and deceive not with your lips. Say not I will do to him the way he has done to me: I will pay the man back for his deed.

SUPPORTING TEXTS = Eph 4:25; Prv 20:22; Matt 5:39,44; Rom 12:17,19.

True witnessing is a requisite concerning words moderation, it is improper to misuse words and commit sins by witnessing falsely against others. It is also improper to use witnessing as a tool of revenge against the adversaries . Offenses committed against the witnesses should be dealt with by God while the witnesses must be upright and honest, while witnessing between people or witnessing by propagating the gospel. Whichever way , there is the requisite to be moderate with the words of witnessing in order not to sin but execute God willed righteousness by true witnessing, and to have the God expected result in the end.

viii = ***SHUNNING GENERIC LIES AND BEING HONEST = (Prv 12:22, AMP).***

Lying lips are extremely disgusting and hateful to the Lord, but they who deal faithfully are his delight.

= (Prv 6:16-17,AMP) =

These six thing does God hates, indeed, seven are abomination to him . V 16. A proud look(the spirit that makes one overestimate himself and underestimate others) a lying tongue, and hands that she'd innocent blood. V 17.

There are various aspect of life affections in which lies manifest. Some people are truthful in some aspects of life, while they are liars in many other areas of life, But some people are inclined to lying all through. Those who are partially liars -partially honest are always driven by circumstances to tell lies, while the inclined {enthusiast} liars chose to possess the habit of lying. Nevertheless; the law of verbal righteousness in this case demands that we should endeavour to be outrightly honest in all aspects of life. It's true that it's not easy to be perfectly honest, yet God wills we should do so because its possible by his grace. Hence we are to strive in all situations to be honest; for when we do so, God by his infinite mercy considers our unfeigned effort to be honest and vindicates our verbal righteousness by consistent honesty. The regular honesty moreover: saves us the from the problems evolving from lies among all of us humans.

ix = *DEFEATING EVIL COUNSELLING WITH GOOD COUNSELLING* = *(Prv 12:20, NAS).*

Deceit is in the hearts of those who device evil , but counsellors of peace have joy.

Immoderate words are revealed through deceitful advises. Therefore, moderate words on the wise manner are truly revealed through good advises. So all advisers in all classes and categories are expected to be consistent and moderate all their words of advise and never to deceive their mentees or clients by counselling but always being upright pertaining to counselling people. When it is done, oral righteousness is displayed by the counsellors. And the peace, clarity and understanding of those they advise are prioritised. The integrity and the reliability with continuity of the advising work of the advisers being stabilised.

x = *DEFEATING REVERSED PSYCHOLOGICAL COMMENTS* = *(Prv 20:14, AMP).*

It is worthless, it is worthless, says the buyer, but when he goes his way, then he boasts(about his bargain).

= (Prv 26:18-19, NAS) =

Like a madman who throws firebrand and death. V 18 So is the man who deceives his neighbour and says, was I not joking? V 19.

= (Isah 5:20 AMPC) =

Woe to those who call evil good and good evil, who put darkness for light and light for darkness, who put bitter for sweet and sweet for bitter!

Some people are crafty by nature and they know many treacherous words to use against others to deceive and manipulate them, in businesses, relationships, group/ team venturing, politics ,religion and much more. In all: the application of crafty words in dealing with others is as a sin of immoderate words, because righteousness requires that lies and all indications of deception must be forbidden by us, as God forbids and abhors deceitful lies of all kinds, and we should endeavour to terminate the crafty nature which erupts crafty words from the minds and pass through the mouths. Because without eliminating crafty words with total honesty, righteousness by honesty is not accepted by God, but when crafty words are perfectly conquered the word of honesty permanently takes over, verbal righteousness through honesty becomes unquestionably accepted by God. The worst is the reversed psychological words that the subtle use to change the games into their own favour and to the misery of their victims. But if the truth be told regularly and permanently and all of us living by it, there Will be no lingering quarrels among us.

xi = DEFEATING FAKE ORAL LOVE WITH PRACTICAL TRUE LOVE = (Prv 26:23-26,28, AMP).

Burning lips(uttering insincere words of love) and a wicked heart are like an earthen vessel covered with the scum thrown off from molten silver(making it appear to be solid silver). V 23. He who hates pretends with his lips, but store up deceit within himself. V 24. When he speaks kindly do not trust him, for seven abominations are in his heart. V 25. Though his hatred hides itself with guile, his wickedness shall be shown openly before the assembly. V 26.

It is abominable in God's sight to pretend to show love to people while negative intentions to hurt them are the real stuffs hoarded in the hearts of the pretentious lovers. But whosoever that should display love for others should do so with pureness and sincerity of heart. Meaning the lovers in question shall love honestly and never intend to dupe, distort from and hurt those they claim to love. Feigned love is truly a sin of duplicity, but otherwise as the study is about moderation, as righteousness; we are responsible for moderating our love for all people, by utterly shunning feigned love, learn to love truly and become devoted to loving people outrightly with alacrity. Because that's the way to truly moderate love in accordance with law of righteousness. This moderation by love are in two aspects which are oral and selfless hospitality.

*xii = **DEFEATING FLATTERING WITH TRUE COMMENDATION** = (Prv 26:28, AMP)*

A lying tongue hates those it wounds and crushes, and a flattering mouth works ruin.

= (Prv 27:14,21, AMP) =

The flatterer who loudly praises and glorifies his neighbour, rising early in the morning, it shall be counted as cursing him (For he will be suspected of sinister purpose). V 14. As the refining pot for silver and furnace for gold(bringing forth all the Impurities of the metal), so let a man be in his trial of praise(riding himself of all that is base or insincere; for a man is judged by what he praises and of what he boasts). V 21.

= (Prv 29:5 AMP) =

A man who flatters his neighbour spreads a net for his own feet.

Treacherous wording and honesty are examples of constructive and destructive words that have decisive influences on humans affairs. people's reputations, fortunes and lives are ruined where God's grace and outright justice do not prevail. There is the need that we don't make ourselves objects of ruination and destruction to others by witnessing falsely against them, tricking them in different ways through the words of our mouths for our selfish gaining, Neither should we orally tarnish the images of others out of hatred, envy and jealousy or talking people down abusively through pride and ostentation. Rather we should moderate how we relate to people by talking and that requires being absolutely honest in all ramifications of talking pertaining to humans matters, while ensuring that all dubious and hate speeches are eliminated from our orations.

xiii = **DEFEATING OSTENTATIOUS COMMENTS WITH GENTLENESS = (Prv 12:23, AMP)**

A prudent man is reluctant to display his knowledge, but the heart of (self confident) fools proclaim their folly.

= (Prv 25:14, AMP) =

Whoever that boasts of gifts (he does not give) is like clouds and wind without rain.

= (Prv 27:1-2, AMP) =

Do not boat of (yourself and)tomorrow for you know not what a day may bring forth. V 1. Let another man praise and not your own mouth; a stranger and not your own lips. V 2.

SUPPORTINGT TEXT = Isa 32:6; Luke 12:19-20; Jms 4:13; Jude :12.

We are required by God to show our wisdom through active humility and self comportment against bragging and show off commenting, because the said are the evidential way of moderating words of ostentation. Rather than nurturing pride which manifests through pompous utterances; we are to be moderate in our words as to refraining totally from wordy pomposity and exhibition of humility and gentleness are typical examples of counter measures to moderating boastfulness. Show off words are sometimes expressed by self exaltation, ego prompted rash vowing, anxiety to display personal knowledge with lack of a sure conviction about the to be displayed knowledge. There are other unlisted ways of expressing verbal pride. Nonetheless, righteousness by moderating words is a divine obligation which should be attained by we humans so to obtain divine grace and justification for success of the earthly and heavenly lives.

*xiv = **EXECUTING FAIR JUDGEMENT** = (Prv 18:5, AMP).*

To respect the person of the wicked and be partial to him so as to deprive (the consistently) righteous is not good.

= (Prv 24:23-25, AMP) =

These also are sayings of the wise; to discriminate and show partiality, having respect of person in judging is not good. V 23. He who says to the wicked you are righteous and innocent, people will curse him, nations will defy and abhor him. V 24. But to those(upright judges) who rebuke the wicked, it will go well with them and they will find delight, and a good blessing will be upon them. V 25.

As it is quite comprehensive that judgements are executed with the words of the mouth. It is also wise that we should be moderate in judging matters between people. This requires that sentiment, nepotism and partiality of all sorts should be despised and forthrightness employed in all cases which need to be judged. Concerning righteousness by word moderation in this aspect: we should not be blinded by tribal, religious, national, ethnic and clannish acquaintances for sentimental preferences to execute false judgements. But we should consistently be impartial in judging between all people so to show ourselves orally moderate and upright before God and man and to find and maintain peace altogether.

DEPENDING ON DIVINE DIRECTION =(Prv 16 1, AMP)

The plans of the mind and orderly thinking belong to man, but from God comes the (wise) answer of the tongue.

We as humans desire to say the right things almost all the time but we constantly fault in our comments due to our natural humans imperfections caused by the distractions of lust, satan and sin. But we have the privilege of prayer through which we demand God inspired guidance of the tongue to enable us rationalise well and talk properly pertaining to all plans, visions, ambitions and responses to people and situations.

Righteousness by words moderation can be inspired, we are therefore obliged to always seek inspiration for word moderation by prayer, by studying God's word accurately and intensely afterwards we should manifest it verbally.

xv = TALKING WITH RATIONALITY AND SAFELY =
(Prv 18:13,20-21, KJV).

He that answereth a matter before he heareth it, it is folly and shame unto him. V 13. A man's belly shall be satisfied with the fruit of his mouth; and with the increase of lips shall he be filled. V 20. Death and life are in the power of the tongue : and they that love it shall eat the fruit thereof. V 21.

= (Prv 29:20, KJV) =

Seest thou a man hasty in his words? There is more hope for a fool than he.

= (Prv 30:30, AMP) =

Do not accuse and hurt a servant before his master, lest he curse you, and you be held guilty(of adding to the burden of the lowly).

SUPPORTING TEXTS = John 7:51; Matt 12:37.

Self condemnation, stupidity at the highest order, slander and various offenses and sins against God are sometimes carelessly committed through irrational utterances. It is therefore proper that, words must be moderated through pre comments rationality. Unlike irrational utterances that leads to offending and sinning; pre comment rationality promotes righteousness of words moderation. Righteousness of words moderation is therefore linked to pre comment rationalising, and law of righteousness proffers rationalising before talking as a divine task to pleasing God. Because, so many precommenting rationality save a lot of lives and difficult circumstances and in some cases it builds the platform for improving life and statuses from the scratch to the top, in favour of the speakers and others. On the opposite way, precommenting irrationality jeopardises the life and statuses including the future and destinies of most irrational speakers and others whom they affect with their irrational and dangerous comments. There is an age long saying that positive confession brings positive possession and negative confession brings negative possession. The texts and explanation of this section affirmatively confirm it. Though our interest is confessing positively and possessing positively.

xvi = *DESPISING SELF JUSTIFICATION WITH GOD'S JUSTIFICATION =(Prv 20:6,9, (AMP).*

Many a man proclaims his own loving kindness and goodness, but a faithful man who can find? V 6 . Who can say I have made my heart clean, I am pure from my sin? V 9.

(Luke 18:10-14 AMPC)

[10] Two men went up into the temple [enclosure] to pray, the one a Pharisee and the other a tax collector. [11] The Pharisee took his stand ostentatiously and began to pray thus before and with himself: God, I thank You that I am not like the rest of men- extortioners (robbers), swindlers [unrighteous in heart and life], adulterers–or even like this tax collector here. [12] I fast twice a week; I give tithes of all that I gain. [13] But the tax collector, [merely] standing at a distance, would not even lift up his eyes to heaven, but kept striking his breast, saying, O God, be favourable (be gracious, be merciful) to me, the especially wicked sinner that I am! [14] I tell you, this man went down to his home justified (forgiven and made upright and in right standing with God), rather

than the other man; for everyone who exalts himself will be humbled, but he who humbles himself will be exalted.

SUPPORTING TEXTS = 1st Kgs 8:46; 2nd Chron 6:36; Job 9:30; Job 14:4; Ps 51:5; 1st John 1:8.

Sins are committed in different ways through self justification which is a product of pride, arrogance and obstinacy, it is hence therefore forbidden by God that it should proceed out of our mouths, but we are to despise oral self justification and depend on God to accept, approve and vindicate all our words and acts acknowledging the fact that, God's justification is authentication of our righteousness by wording. Anybody like the Pharisees can claim to be right in and qualified for whatever but only God has the real justification which he extracts from his own principles and standards for any word and act. So for anyone to be truly justified in anything he or she must surrender to God's justification for him or her. Having known this, we should focus on saying and doing the things which God approves, and be willing and ready to amend whenever we realise the things we say and do which God disapproves.

xvii = DESPISING SELF RIGHTEOUSNESS WITH GOD'S RIGHTEOUSNESS =(Prv 20:6,9, AMP).

Many a man proclaims his own loving kindness and goodness, but a faithful man who can find? V 6. Who can say I have made my heart clean, I am pure from my sin? V 9.

= (Prv 16:25, KJV) =

There is a way that seemeth right unto a man, but the end thereof are ways of death.

= (Prv 14:12, KJV) =

There is a way which seemeth right unto a man, but the end thereof are ways of death.

= (Matt 5:20 AMPC) =

For I tell you, unless your righteousness (your uprightness and your right standing with God) is more than that of the scribes and Pharisees, you will never enter the kingdom of heaven.

SUPPORTING TEXTS =

1st Kgs 8:46; 2nd Chron 6:36; Job 9:30; Job 14:4; Ps 51:5; 1st John 1:8 .

Self righteousness and self justification are two hold products of human nature which evolve obstinacy and reprobation through which repentance to obtaining salvation becomes impossible. But God's righteousness and God's justification functions otherwise because God's righteousness is attained through absolute godly humility, and God's justification results in God's righteousness for the holy humble person. Hence oral moderation to exhibiting righteousness demands that, wording self righteousness must be utterly overcome with God's proclaimed righteousness upon those who dare live for God's pleasure. Therefore there is the need to shun self vindication in all ramifications of life and walk vehemently to obtain the real vindication which God institutes for those who love him and live for him. We must be saying exactly what God says to be right for us to be verbally righteous. And we must be doing exactly what God does and requires us to do for us to be attitudinally righteous.

xviii = DEMOTING CURSING BY BLESSING = (Prv 20:20, KJV)

Whoever curses his father or his mother, his lamp shall be put out in complete darkness .

= (Gen 12:1, 3 AMPC) =

[1] NOW [in Haran] the Lord said to Abram, Go for yourself [for your own advantage] away from your country, from your relatives and your father's house, to the land that I will show you. [Heb. 11:8-10.]. [3] And I will bless those who bless you [who confer prosperity or happiness upon you] and curse him who curses or uses insolent language toward you; in you will all the families and kindred of the earth be blessed [and by you they will bless themselves]. [Gal. 3:8.]

(Jms 3:5-6, 8-12 AMPC)

[5] Even so the tongue is a little member, and it can boast of great things. See how much wood or how great a forest a tiny spark can set ablaze! [6] And the tongue is a fire. [The tongue is a] world of wickedness set among our members, contaminating and depraving the whole body and setting on fire the wheel of birth (the cycle of man's nature), being itself ignited by hell (Gehenna). [8] But the human tongue can be tamed by no man. It is a restless (undisciplined, irreconcilable) evil, full of deadly poison. [9] With it we bless the Lord and Father, and with it we curse men who were made in God's likeness! [10] Out of the same mouth come forth blessing and cursing. These things, my brethren, ought not to be so. [11] Does a fountain send forth [simultaneously] from the same opening fresh water and bitter? [12] Can a fig tree, my brethren, bear olives, or a grapevine figs? Neither can a salt spring furnish fresh water.

Parents are hereby used as a cases example of those we are to bless rather than cursing them, as it seems wise that we should be wise children of our immediate earthly parents, all other male and female elders who are as old as being our parents, and those older than them mostly the ones with good parental virtues. By Christian faith, we are to honour our spiritual mentors and mentoresses, which are those rightly chosen by God to spearhead the running of the church, more especial when they are leading the church on the narrow way and track to salvation and into God's Kingdom. And we are under obligation to bless God and we have no reason to curse him, because he is ever perfect that he never offended us and will never offend us. We are also required to bless all other humans, more especially those who are innocent toward us. We are not to curse people unnecessarily, because cursing unnecessarily is a sin while blessing accordingly is a righteousness exhibited by word moderation.

CONTROLLING EMOTIONS.

DEFINITION = The ability to discipline thoughts, feelings in play or never to display them.

MEMORY VERSE = {Gen 6:6 AMPC} = *And the Lord regretted that He had made man on the earth, and He was grieved at heart.*

(John 11:35 AMPC) = Jesus wept.

INTRODUCTION

Life of discipline is universally related to all kinds of actions, inactions, reactions and behaviours, of which all form the derivation of the term {emotions}. Most people were absolutely ignorant of the fact that, humans reckless actions, inactions and comments are projected by our emotions, but due to the internet floods of revelational insights over it nowadays, many of us have easy access to the knowledge and can confidently confirm the authenticity of it. Emotions are so effective in the positive or negative manifestations, and the positive manifestation of emotions are advantageous while the negative manifestation of it is disadvantageous. In this lesson you will see some examples of emotions people exhibit either in the positive or in the negative ways, how they do it and how the results from them prove their effects whether of advantages or of disadvantages. Anger, agony, regret, jealousy, envy, kind or hostile words, humility and pride, hunger, contentment, greed, anxiety, and so on are some of the examples of emotions. Mismanaging each of them is a way of being emotionally immoderate in that area, while managing each of them well is a means of moderating emotions in that area of emotion. Moreover: self control over all sorts of emotions is the utmost requirement in our dealings with emotions, and the lesson is formed to give some deep explanations of how to control emotions and to produce global benefits through that control.

---

i = DEFEATING ENVY AND JEALOUSY WITH RIGHTEOUS ACTIVITIES = (Prv 3:31-32, KJV)

Envy thou not the oppressor, and choose None of his ways. V 31. For the froward is abomination to the lord: But his secret is with the righteous. V 32.

= (Prv 23:17-18, KJV) =

Let not thine heart envy sinners: but be thought in the fear of the Lord all the day long. V 17. For surely there is an end, and thine expectation shall not be cut off. V 18.

= (Prv 24:1-2, KJV) =

Be thou not envious against evil men, neither desire To be with them. V 1. For their heart studieth destruction and their lips talk Of mischief. V 2 .

SUPPORTING TEXTS = Ps 25:14; Ps 37:1; Ps 73:3.

Most of the time after having being faithful to God it seem that the ungodly are far more prosperous, successful and comfortable, to the extent the that faithful begin envying the ungodly and ultimately become jealous of them. Or in some cases the godly begin desiring to be like the supposed comfortable sinners, in times of illicit venturing and livelihoods and sensuality. If not by the overcoming grace of God: the righteous will definitely deviate from the track of true godliness and join the ways of the ungodly with the intents of becoming like them or surpassing them in worldly ventures, wealth possession and comforts. But we are hereby forewarned to moderate our emotions which is to be exemplified by not being moved by sight but always being moved by godly faith to focused on God's timing and ability to perform that which he has promised to those who love him and are vehemently conformed to his commands and statutes. Hence the Christian believers are to focus on executing acceptable personal conducts and generally faithful services to God and all humanity for which God will be pleased to reward them accordingly here on earth and in heaven, because their works reveal righteousness by moderation of envy and jealousy to continuing in good works. In addition the righteous must advance from mediocrity to engage in excellent and righteous ventures through which they can have advanced prosperity. And by doing so, they may not have the time and attention to be obsessed with contemplating on the prosperity of the wicked. Most Christians likewise non Christians are envious and jealous of others just because they (the jealous and envious) are mediocres who refuse to strive for excellence, but are jealousing the affluent but ungodly people.

*ii = **MODERATING REPROVING** = (Prv 9:7-9, NAS).*

He who corrects a scoffer gets dishonour for himself, and he who reprove a wicked man gets insult for himself. V 7. Do not reprove a scoffer, or he will hate you, reprove a wise man and hew will love you. V 8. Give instruction to a wise man and he will be still wiser, teach a righteous man and he will increase in learning. V 9.

= (Prv 27:5, NAS) =

Better is open rebuke than love that is concealed.

= (Prv 28:23, NAS) =

He who rebukes a man shall afterwards find favour than he who flatters with his tongue.

SUPPORTING TEXT = Ps 141:5; Gal 2:14.

The teachable and the scornful arrogant are the two major sets of people under the responsibility of the correctors to guide and educate. But discernment is necessary in the work of correcting people from their misconducts. For without the discerning to invest correction rightly, the correctors will continue to struggle with some of those whom they mean well for by trying to correct them. Because there are sets of people who hate learning and correcting their errors but prefer persisting in their awkward lifestyle, while otherwise some sets of people love learning and correcting their errors and mistakes. So in the process to correct the arrogant (those who resist learning and being corrected but prefer progressing in their errors) by all menaces the correctors are being hated and insulted by the arrogant and while quarrelling with the arrogant the correctors commit sins through grievances.

Nevertheless: discernment enables the correctors to divert from the arrogant and channel all of their energy and corrective measures to the teachable(those willing to learn and be corrected) so that the correctors save themselves from distresses, quarrels, insolency and hatred from the arrogant and in the same vein the correctors secure, gratitude, love, respect and tranquillity for themselves; by abandoning the impenetrable arrogant and concentrate in dealing with the accessible teachable ones. Because that is how to execute righteousness by moderating reproving.

iii CONTROLLING SEXUAL URGE = (Prv 5:15-20, AMP).

Drink waters out of your own cistern (of a pure marriage relationship), and fresh running waters out of your own well. V 15. Should your offspring be dispersed abroad as water brooks in the streets? V16. (Confine yourself to your own wife) let your children be for you alone, and not the children of strangers with you. V 17. Let your fountain(of human life) be blessed(with rewards of fidelity), and rejoice in the wife of your youth. V 18. Let her be as loving hind and pleasant doe(tender, gentle attractive - let her bosom satisfy you at all times, and always be transported with delight in her love. V 19. Why should you, my son, be infatuated with a loose woman, embrace the bosom of an outsider and go astray? 20.

SUPPORTING TEXTS = Ps 19:18; Ps 109:105; Prv 5:3-8; Prv 6:23-26; Prv 9:13-18; Prv 31:1-4; Eccl 10:17; Ezek 20:30; Hos 4:11; Col 12:8-10; Rom 16:17; 1st Thes 5:19-22; Gal 5:18-21; 2nd Pet 2:14-17.

Contentment is required to moderating sexual urge. Sexual urge is an untamed emotion in the lives in which contentment is lacking. As contentment is needed in material acquisition so it is in the desire to have sex. Sex is truly made for married couples, while all pre marital and extramarital sex are sin. Homosexuality and bestiality are more sinful than fornication, adultery and incest, because the laters are between a man and a woman while the farmers are either between a man with a fellow man or between two women in sex.

In this aspect it is required that sex life must be moderated in order to not defile self and sin against God through sex. Therefore there is an obligation to be self disciplined pertaining to sex life, and the disciplinary actions for sex is impracticable without the application of contentment for sex. It's quite obvious that, sex drive and persistent craving to having sex is not easy to be controlled but God makes it possible by his grace. So we are to possess and exhibit fear of God in our sexual life. This simply means that, the married should concentrate on their life partners alone for sex while the unmarried are to be absolutely out of sex until they're married, then be sexually faithful to their personal partners or live forever as celibates. That is what needs to be done to moderate sexual urge and it's practices, which preserves sexual integrity and dignity and righteousness by moderating sexual urge.

iv = CONQUERING HATRED WITH LOVE = (Prv 10:12, NAS) =

Hatred stirs up strife but love covers all transgressions.

= (Prv 14:20, NAS) =

The poor is hated even by his neighbour but those who love the rich are many.

SUPPORTING TEXTS = 1st John 3:15; 1st John 4:20.

Hatred for others can erupt from being often offended by them, it can also result from, envy and jealousy by different segments of peoples, and individual to individual. It can also occur as a result of some people's poverty and insignificance, the insignificant poor who are agitated with seeing the significant and the rich gallivanting with their splendours. Many poor are hated, despised and ignored by others due to their penury and insignificant lives, while the rich are loved and in end are followed by many due to their opulence and social status, with expectations of their supporters to get some favours from them. There are others who love the poor not by pitying them because of their economic condition but because of their good reputation, or they get some favours or they expect to get favoured by the poor. There are other reasons to hate or love anybody, but the emphatic point here is the fact that each person in this world is hated by some people and the same person being loved by some other people for any reasons.

Hence hating and despising the poor, because of their poverty and loving and cherishing the rich because of expecting favour from them; is a sin of relational sentiment caused by biasedness. But moderating the emotion which drive people to sentimentally hate the poor and love the rich is necessary in this aspect of life, and it is practicable by endeavouring to love the poor as well as to love the rich and not to exhibit hatred for any, and never for any selfish motive. For God is love and wills that we human who are created in his image should like him perfectly, love one another regardless of their classes.

*v = **CONQUERING VERBOSITY WITH DILIGENT CALMING** = (Prv 17:27-28, KJV).*

He that hath Knowledge spareth his words: and a man of understanding is of an excellent spirit. V 27. Even a fool, when he holdeth his peace, is counted wise: And he that shutteth his lips is esteemed a man of understanding. V 28

= (Prv 20:19, KJV) =

He that goes about as a tale bearer revealeth secrets: therefore meddle not with him that flattereth with his lips.

= (Prv 29:20, AMP) =

Do you see a man hasty in his words? There is hope for a (Self confident) fool than him.

People are easily beguiled through too much of talking, the talking may be prompted by excitement to display personal knowledge and eloquence or by delighting in telling of stories about self and others: and the talkatives talk rashly, stupidly and offensively thereby. Ironically the prudent dare withhold their words even at some points that they know the right things to say and can orally and skillfully showcases their mights about certain issues; all because the prudent understand the powers of words and that words contain offenses and sins when they are misapplied. Hence it's wise to restrain from verbosity and prefer being silent at times, respite we have the knowledge of the points of discussions and occurrences which develop the discussions, just to moderate words and display the necessary verbal righteousness.

vi = DEFEATING PREJUDICE WITH ACCURATE VERIFICATIONS =
(Prv 18:13, AMP)

He who answers a matter before he hears the facts – It is folly and shame to him.

= (Prv 19:2, AMPC) =

Desire without knowledge is not good, and to be overhasty is to sin and miss the mark.

= (Prv 29:20, AMP) =

Do you see a man who is hasty in his words? There is more hope for a (self confident) fool than for him.

= (Prv 30:10, AMP) =

Do not accuse and hurt a servant before his master, lest he curse you and you be held guilty (of adding to the burdens of the lowly).

SUPPORTING TEXT = John 7:15.

Prejudicing and responding to things by wording have ensnared many people in different ways. Verbal response by prejudice is a sin causing foolishness. it is therefore wise that responses should not hinge on vague conclusions. We are to be prudent in responding to all matters regardless of the circumstances attached to the matters on which we should speak. We are also to be discrete in approaching every affairs so to not err by the words of our mouths. Therefore we are responsible for tracing the root cause of every affection which we are to judge or determine about it in some ways. The same thing is applicable to humans whom we happen to judge or decide their affairs. The responsibility of verification before uttering decisions and judgements is essential. Because failing to do so always result in erroneous judging and concluding, justifying the offenders and condemning the offended, justifying the guilt and condescending the innocent. That is a sin of prejudice, but moderating judgemental words is evident in conquering prejudice with proper findings with assurance and thus the determiners or judges can execute righteousness by words moderation. Beside judgement prejudicial words can manifest in witnessing, gossiping, flattery, commendations, and much more through which the prejudicing people underestimate or exaggerate their comments on those they speak against and those they favour.

*vii = **DEFEATING ANXIETY WITH GODLY DILIGENCE =**
(19:1-2, AMP).*

Better is a poor man who walks in his integrity than a rich man who was is perverse in his speech and is a(self confident) fool. V 1. Desire without knowledge is not good, and to be over hasty is to sin and miss the mark. V 2.

= (Prv 25:8-10, AMP) =

Rush not too soon to quarrel (before magistrates or elsewhere, lest you know not what to do in the end when your neighbour has put you to shame. V 8. Argue your cause with your neighbour himself: discover not and disclose not another's secrets. V 9. Lest he who hears you revile you and bring shame upon you and your ill repute has no end . V 10.

SUPPORTING TEXT = Matt 5:24,39,44; Matt 6:31-34; Matt 18:15; Rom 12:17,19; Eph 4:25.

Anxiety is one of the humans shortcomings which lead to practical ungodly impatience and making costly and ruinous mistakes. Anxiety itself is a sin while expression it elaborates the sin of it. The remedy for anxiety is godly diligence and patience. Therefore godly diligence is required to moderate between anxiety and patience. It is also necessary to study principles of perfect godliness through which the insight of godly diligence is obtained; because exercising godly patience is impossible in the absence of God inspired diligence. Anxiety is emotional hastiness for achieving desired or essential things, while godly diligence is emotional calmness with precaution for achieving desired essentials without mistaking.

Anxiety manifests verbally by being hasty to report matters against speculated offenders while the anxious reporter will be ignorant of their personal offenses until they are truly proved wrong. It also manifest in desperation to desires by which the expectants tell lies in order to attain their selfish profits and favours in almost all venturing they are engaged. Anxiety is an emotional cancer destroying humans affections and leaving many ill fated. It also triggers prejudicing in the life of its subjects. But social diligence makes people to be rational and discrete before speaking or acting, while godly diligence helps people the be excellent with rationality and discretion and in control of situations and to perform excellently.

viii = **DEMOTING RASH DESIRES WITH PRUDENCE** =
(Prv 19:2, AMP).

Desire without knowledge Is not good, and to be over hasty is to sin and miss the mark .

It is very common among people to crave various sorts of things without realising the costs of getting or achieving them, and at the same time not to realise the consequences of obtaining their rash desires, whether they shall be good or bad. Nevertheless: it is right to be discerning while desiring for things reason being that, selfish desiring is a sin, and unselfish desiring a kind of righteousness: Hence prudence is a necessity regarding to desires so to moderate desiring by being rational and not to sin by evil desiring and its negative outcomes and to show forth righteousness by ensuring that all of desires are in line with the will of God whereupon law of principles of righteousness lie.

ix = CONQUERING CARNAL ANGER WITH TOLERANCE =
(Prv 14:29, NAS).

He who is slow to anger has great understanding, but he who is quick tempered exalts folly.

= (Prv 16:32, NAS) =

He who is slow to anger is better than the mighty, And he who rules his spirit than he who captures a city.

= (Prv 19:11, NAS) =

A man's discretion make him slow to anger, And it is his glory to overlook a transgression.

= (Prv 17:14, NAS) =

The beginning of a strife is like letting out of water, so abandon the quarrel before it breaks out.

= (Prv 20:2-3,22, NAS) =

The terror of a king is like the glowing of a lion; He who provokes him to anger forfeits his own life. V 2. Keeping away from strife is an honour to a man, But any fool will quarrel. V 3. Do not say I will repay evil, wait for the Lord, he will save you. V 22.

= (Prv 24:28-29, NAS) =

Do not be a witness against your neighbour without cause, and do not deceive with thy lips. V 28. Do not say thus, I shall do to him as he has done to me, I will render to the man according to his work. V 29.

= (Prv 29:11, NAS) =

A fool always loses his temper, but a wise man holds it back.

= (Prv 30:33, NAS) =

For the churning of the milk produces butter, and pressing the nose brings forth blood; So the churning of anger produces strife.

SUPPORTING TEXTS =

Matt 5:14,39,44; Matt 18:15; Rom 12:17,19-20 ; Eph 4:25; Jms 1:19.

Tolerance is a key factor in the Christian walk and services to God and entirety of humanity. For without tolerance anger will be absolutely untamed in the lives of the Christian believers whom are divinely assigned to live in modesty; as a part of the light to the corrupt world, and are to add flavour which is typified by salt to the world. This means possessing and exhibiting uncommon positive attributes of which being tolerant is one.

All the said are intended to be applied to moderate temper, as it is understood that, undisciplined anger definitely lure its victims into foolish reactions to provocations, and thereby commit sins of rash responses, actions and reactions.

Sometimes untamed anger leads its victims to utter false witnessing as a means of revenge against their offenders. In some occasions anger manifests as a result of intolerance rising from strong ego and persistence to protect it against any challenger. But whichever way, uncontrolled anger stupefies it's victims and consistently lures them to sinning in different ways. So to moderate temper; one has to display maturity, which must be evident in the ability to forbear offenses when necessary, and to demonstrate righteousness by depending on God for avenging on our behalves concerning our offenders.

x = *MODERATING VOWING BY SHUNNING RASH SURETYING =*
(Prv 20:16, AMP).

(The judge tells the creditor) Take the garment of one who is a security for a stranger; and hold him in pledge when he is security for foreigner.

There is no wisdom and righteousness for suretying for the interests of others and only to regret doing so when being held responsible to pay for the depth of the borrowers who fail to pay what they are suretyed for. It is also foolishness and sin to stake personal belongings for suretying others and later regret doing it because the borrowers whom are suretyed cannot pay for what they borrowed. But it is wisdom and righteousness to moderate words of suretying by refraining from rash suretying; meaning that it is better to keep calm and not to be involved in the bargains which include suretying others than offending self and stupidly offending God and the offender inherits agony in the end, in addition to his or her sin by rash suretying. Being moderate with and being free from suretying others while in emotional hastiness can be possible by the potential surety thinking to discern his or her ability to bear the consequences of the suretyship, or he's not able to bear it. And to go on to surety if he's or she's able or to refuse to surety if he's / she's unable.

xi = SHUNNING RASH VOWING WITH PRECAUTION = (Prv 20:25, AMP)

It is a snare to a man to utter a vow (of consecration rashly and (not until) afterward inquire (whether he can fulfill it).

= (Eccl 5:2-5, AMPC) =

[2] Be not rash with your mouth, and let not your heart be hasty to utter a word before God. For God is in heaven, and you are on earth; therefore let your words be few. [3] For a dream comes with much business and painful effort, and a fool's voice with many words. [4] When you vow a vow or make a pledge to God, do not put off paying it; for God has no pleasure in fools (those who witlessly mock Him). Pay what you vow. [Ps. 50:14; 66:13, 14; 76:11.] [5] It is better that you should not vow than that you should vow and not pay. [Prov. 20:25; Acts 5:4.]

The vow of personal sacredness is hereby used as an example to promote moderation of vowing. The vow makers are to be prudent with any vow they're to declare; because sins of vowing erupt from rash vowing, as the people in question fail to realise the costs of the vows they intend to make and fail to accomplish what they have vowed for, due to their inability to pay the costs. The vow of Nazarene is the key factor while material pledging are secondary. Which ever ones, vowing but not fulfilling exposes lack of honesty and integrity, anxiety and foolishness of the vowers. At the same time leading them into rebelling against God and dishonouring him.

But righteousness by vowing and words moderation is prompted by the ability to apply discretion before vowing so to be able to afford the moral and material prices of meeting the vows or to save words and not vowing when it is discerned that the potent to meet the vows are lacking in the life and capabilities of the vow makers.

xii = DISCIPLINNING EATING AND DRINKING APPETITES =
(Prv 15:16-17, KJV).

Better is little with the fear of God than great treasure and trouble therewith. V 16. Better is a dinner of herb where love is, than a stalled ox and hatred therewith. V 17.

= (Prv 23:1-3,6-8, KJV) =

When thou sittest to eat with a ruler, consider diligently what is before thee. V 1. And out a knife to throat, if thou be a man given to appetite. V 2. Be thou not desirous of dainties, for they are deceitful meat. V 3. Be thou not the bread of him that hath an evil eye, Neither desire thou his dainty meat. V 6. For as he thinketh in his heart, so is he: eat and drink saith he to thee; but his heart Is not with thee. V 7. The morsel which thou hast eaten shalt thou vomit up, and lose thy sweet words. V 8.

It is good to be sensitive concerning what to eat and what to drink. It should be unwise to be ensnared by food and drinks irrespective of the urge, situations and enticements which should be the causes for not discerning properly before eating or drinking anything offered. It is wise and right if the eaters should moderate their appetite by endeavouring to be self controlled to eating and drinking, so they should not fall for enticing foods and drinks, eat excessively, abusively, offensively and sinfully. The eaters should consistently be prudent to realise the kinds of food and drinks given to them by their purported, givers / philanthropists. And hence the evil intentions of the presumed cheerful givers are unfolded through their (supposed beneficiaries) discernment. The eaters should therefore execute righteousness by refraining from emotional drive to eat and drink out of normality, and better refusing the enticing food and drinks offers than to stupefy themselves and commit sin of emotional indiscipline thereby.

*xiii = **TALKING PRUDENTLY** = (Prv 13:16, AMP)*

Every prudent man deals with knowledge, but a (self confident) fool exposes and flaunts his folly

= (Prov 18:2 AMPC) =

A [self-confident] fool has no delight in understanding but only in revealing his personal opinions and himself.

= (Prov 26:4-5 AMPC) =

[4] Answer not a [self-confident] fool according to his folly, lest you also be like him. [5] Answer a [self-confident] fool according to his folly, lest he be wise in his own eyes and conceit. [Matt. 16:1-4; 21:24-27.]

Emotions are able to determine people's behaviours when they are in or out of self control. Lack of self control or self discipline erupts stupid and sinful behaviours . Notwithstanding: There is the need to be persistently self Comported in the presences of sudden happenings. Whether the happenings are good or bad, it is necessarily righteous for one to comport himself/herself and not be distracted by whatsoever emotions to misbehave and sin thereby.

We cannot stop some certain things from happening, likewise we cannot stop certain people from behaving how they behave but we can discipline ourselves to responding appropriately to the happenings and the people. The fools with their persistent foolish acts are recklessly provocative and how the prudent respond intelligently to them are the key contexts. Being opinionated and saucy is one of the characteristic identities of the fools, so we are to have it at the back of our minds that they're unwilling for rationality and prevalence of superior views. So we must be moderate with how we respond to them. And to do so requires us to be so intelligent to know when to talk to or with them and when not, and to always respond cautiously and wisely when necessary.

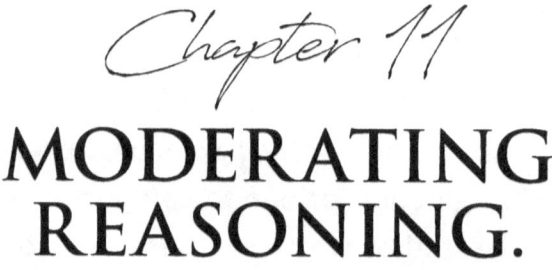

MODERATING REASONING.

DEFINITION = 1 = Balancing the equation of thinking, personal perspectives and counter thoughts and perspectives as personal or from others.

2 = Advancing from humans standpoints to God's standpoints for everything.

MEMORY VERSE = *Prov 3:7 NKJV = Do not be wise in your own eyes; Fear the Lord and depart from evil.*

= Prov = 12:15 NKJV =

The way of a fool is right in his own eyes, But he who heeds counsel is wise.

INTRODUCTION

Being over righteous is a sin likewise being not up to righteous is a sin. We are therefore instructed to be moderate in everything we do so we can be contented therein and reasoning is not exceptional from the episodes.

Eccl 7:16-18, NKJV = [16] Do not be overly righteous, Nor be overly wise: Why should you destroy yourself? [17] Do not be overly wicked, Nor be foolish: Why should you die before your time? [18] It is good that you grasp this, And also not remove your hand from the other; For he who fears God will escape them all.

Moderation and contentment about everything are the two key principles of Righteousness and wisdom. The inability to moderate reasoning is the major cause of becoming an opinionated fool. But the ability to moderate reasoning is the major cause of becoming a discrete. Immoderation of everything is repercussive while moderation of everything is beneficial. However: we are to realise the fact that moderation does not mean compromise. Therefore there should be no misplaced priority in the exercise of moderation leading to contentment. This lesson focuses on being contented in reasoning by moderating the reasoning processes. So you should be looking into the principles of being moderate and contented with reasons, the repercussions of not doing so, and the benefits of doing them.

i = PRE ACTING RATIONALISING = (Prv 13:16, AMP).

Every prudent man deals with knowledge, but a (self confident)fool exposes and flaunt his folly.

It is unwise and evil to be the self confident fool who flaunts through misbehaving as the text unveils; But wisdom and righteousness by personal behaviour is seen in the prudent comportment of the truly moral disciplined individuals, who think to realise the consequences before they speak or act and to try as much as possible to avoid messing themselves up by their own comments and actions.

It is therefore good that the good morals should continue in their prudent lifestyle which is founded on good rationality and the mediocre and teachable morals follow suit in the steps of the prudent morals and not to learn from the foolish and irrational immoral. Because; emulating the irrational and foolish immoral only tend to misbehaving and singing thereby; but learning the ways of the prudent tend to behaving rightly and be qualified to obtain the God's grace of justification for righteousness for reasoning well and behaving well. Irrational comments and irrational acts bring self shame and degradation but rationally prudent comments and acts bring honour and reliability.

ii = BEING COOL TEMPERED = (Prv 15:18, AMP).

A hot tempered man stirs up strife, but he who is slow to anger appeases contention.

= (16:32, AMP) =

He who is slow to anger is better than the mighty, he who rules his spirit than he who takes a city.

= (Prov 17:12, 14 NKJV) =

[12] Let a man meet a bear robbed of her cubs, Rather than a fool in his folly. [14] The beginning of strife is like releasing water; Therefore stop contention before a quarrel starts.

= (Prv 19:19, AMP) =

A man of great wrath shall suffered the penalty; for If you deliver him (from the consequences),he will(feel free to) cause you to do it again.

SUPPORTING TEXT = Hos 13:8.

Controlling personal temper is one of the proves of behavioural maturity, Christian spiritual growth, and righteousness by self discipline. We are to comprehend that we are living in the world full of offenses which are to distract the Christians from focusing on their Kingdom services and race to eternal life, which are the focal essences of their calling. The earthly distracting offenses are also tools of hindrances to the feeble minded and unrefined believers of Christ, from responding, serving properly and pursuing their eternal lives in righteousness. Therefore we should endeavour to overcome offenses by moderating our temper which should be impracticable in the absence of forbearance and leading of the holy spirit. Hence forbearance and the holy spirit are essential in the life of those who will definitely moderate their temper and be victorious as exhibitors of righteousness by being calmly tempered. In regards to reasoning: conceitedness is the fundamental factor to being rude and feeling being challenged by the people of counter reasons and perspectives. I discovered that most of the ill tempered people are so not because people offended them every now and then, but because they conclude everything to be right and wise based on their own understanding of it and never have avenue for objections. In this case the conceited ill-tempered regard all objectors as foolish argumentators whose foolish arguments must be dealt with together with them the objectors. The irrational hot tempered fight to subdue their objectors rather than reasoning with them to prove them wrong or to accept their own views and opinions if they're right and better. But for us to be moderate and contented with our temper, we must be rational and reasonable to admitting our flaws and surrender to superior reasons and facts. More so we must be willing to let go of many offenses and to be preventive to foreseen offenses as much as possible.

iii = *CONQUERING PRIDE AND EGO WITH HUMILITY =*
    (Prv 18:12).

Haughtiness comes before disaster, but humility before honour.

= *(Jms 4:6-7 NKJV) =*

[6] But He gives more grace. Therefore He says: "God resists the proud, But gives grace to the humble." [7] Therefore submit to God. Resist the devil and he will flee from you.

Lustful pride and ego is a sin while godly humility is righteousness, therefore moderating between humility and pride with ego, it is necessary to eradicate all sorts of pride and arrogant self esteem in life and ensure that humility is put in manifestation and to God and not to ungodly humans or demons. So rather than being conquered by pride and ego we are responsible to conquer pride and ego by being absolutely loyal to God and his laws of righteousness through which righteousness by moderating personal conduct is authenticated. Divine demotion and humiliation are parts of the repercussions of carnal pride and ego.

iv = *CONQUERING REPROBATION WITH GODLY TEACHABLENESS = (Prv 19:16, AMP).*

He who keeps the commandments (of the lord)keeps his own life, but he who despises his ways shall die.

= (Prv 21:3,27, NAS) =

To do righteousness and justice is desired by the Lord than sacrifice. V 3. The sacrifice of the wicked is an abomination, how much more when he brings it with evil intent. V 27.

SUPPORTING TEXTS = Luke 10:28; Luke 11:28; 1st Sam 15:22-23; Isa 1:11; Hos 6:6; Mic 6:6-7.

Reprobation is; a combination of self will, arrogance and unrepentance in manifestation, and such is a sin. The preference of giving money, other materials and unacceptable zealous services to God and the church in replacement of godly obedience: are typical proofs of acts of reprobation, but to moderate conducts from reprobation there should be a total surrender of self will, lusts and self righteousness to the will and righteousness of God without which the exhibition of godly obedience in not possible. Moreover: the inability to submit to God is the inability to moderate self and be contented in him. It is moreso an expression of rejecting God and God in return rejects the reprobate. Having said so: We must moderate our relationship with God by we humbling ourselves to his teachings, reproves and corrections and to have our space into his heart and to be honourably favoured by him.

v = RELYING ON DIVINE DIRECTIONS = (Prv 16:9, AMP).

A man's mind plans his way, but the Lord directs his steps and make them sure.

(Prv 20:24, AMP)

Man's steps are ordered by the Lord, how then can a man understand his ways?

SUPPORTING TEXTS = Ps 37:23; Ps 119:96-105; Jer 10:23.

For by arms flesh shall no man prevail. We as natural humans can struggle to live up to God's demand in behaving modestly but the fact is that we cannot truly live up to God required perfect righteousness by personal behaviours except we are upheld by the grace of God for self discipline and by walking in the guiding light of God's word and various ways of divine mentoring. For certain, no one can truly moderate his or her conduct when divine directives are lacking in his life. So it is important to depend on God and his principles and grace through the holy Spirit, hence consistently pray to receive them and be sustained by them, so to perfectly moderate personal conducts and show forth righteousness thereby. Relying on God's directions and living by them not only mould our good conduct, they also lead to living a victorious life in every respect.

vi = CONQUERING DUPLICITY WITH UPRIGHTNESS = (Prv 21:7-8, AMP).

The violence of the wicked shall sweep them away, because they refuse to do justice. V 7.

The way of the crooked is exceedingly crooked, but as for the pure, his work Is right and his conduct is straight. V 8.

Duplicity is a product of human nature and it's an evidential sin. But in pursuing righteousness by moderating personal conduct; there is the obligation to truly conquer natural treachery by endeavouring with personal efforts and obtained divine grace to be upright in all respects of life and it's affections. Without overcoming our natural trickery we can never be upright with God and our fellow humans. The both of treachery and uprightness are conflicting seeds which bring abundant returns to whoever sows them just like every other positive or negative emotions and attitudes do. The effects of treachery and uprightness get to others whom we express them to and they reflect as aftermaths to us who exhibit them. There are also others who are affected by the effects just because they're connected to us, to our victims and our beneficiaries from the treachery or the uprightness. In conclusion we are required to be moderate and contented with the life of uprightness and to eradicate treachery of all kinds, for us to be blessings and not courses to ourselves and to others.

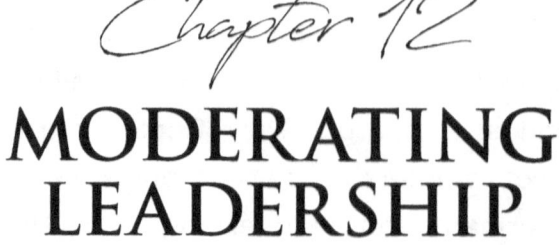

MODERATING LEADERSHIP

DEFINITION = 1 = Leading by carrying everyone along and ensuring that, good interests and wellbeing of each person is secure.

2 = Being a selfless, righteous and kind leader.

MEMORY VERSE = *Prov 29:21 NKJV = [21] He who pampers his servant from childhood Will have him as a son in the end.*

INTRODUCTION

There is a probability that everyone should be a leader sometimes and in different categories. Though on my own conviction I assert there is the certainty that everyone must be or become a leader sometimes. My reason is that as all humans are growing from their childhood, they begin to have younger people as their siblings or not over who they can have some privilege of authority and control. Guardians of the children are their leaders. School teachers are leaders of the pupils and students. school classes prefects are leaders of the school/class mates. The school principals are the utmost school leaders. Parents are the leaders of their own children, kings are community leaders. Politicians are regional and national leaders. There are leaders in the commerce and industry sectors. I'm not forgetting to mention the church and the religious leaders. Even in sports we have the team management, the coaches, the captains and so on. Leaders have dominant authority and influence over the people. So the system of any leadership determines the state of affairs of the majority whether good or bad, everywhere in the world. The situation of the world today is sourced from leadership. This lesson is drafted for revealing how leadership can be made fair and how it can benefit everyone. The reason will also be hinting of the negative effects of bad leadership.

---

i = LEADING WITH PERSONAL INTEGRITY = (Prv 16:12, KJV).

It is an abomination for a king to commit wickedness, for the throne is established by righteousness.

When personal integrity is a top priority to a leader he or she ensures that the leadership thrives goodly so that his reputation will not be marred. In the process of protecting the integrity and good reputation the leaders try to prove themselves to be innocent in their leadership and by so doing they endeavour to be moderate with all of their leadership undertakings.

ii = LEADING IN RIGHTEOUSNESS = (Prv 29:2,12, KJV).

When the righteous are in authority, the people rejoice: But when the wicked beareth rule: the people mourn. V 2.

In the right sense leaders should be God's representatives who must make the policies and Will of God for the people the pivotal subject matter. It's unfortunate that most leaders don't acknowledge God and his purpose, and they never regard themselves and the entire humans to be Gods own super properties that must be led and cared for according to how God wants it. For leading in the will of God which is evident in promoting the welfare of the subjects and preserving personal integrity and good reputation, the leaders are models of righteousness emanating from contentment.

iii = GIVING CAUTIOUS ATTENTION TO ALL = (Prov 29:12 NKJV).

If a ruler pays attention to lies, All his servants become wicked.

= (Prov 20:26 NKJV) =

[26] A wise king sifts out the wicked, And brings the threshing wheel over them.

Every great person is surrounded by many sycophants, whether it's obvious or obscure. The sycophants are busybodies who go about seeking faults of others whom they will gossip and slander to bring them down for their own recognition and upliftment. It's more especially when they realise those who gossip or cheat the great person in some matters, the sycophants use them to buy favour from the great. A typical example are those who set Daniel and the three Hebrew friends [Shedarach, Meshach and Abednego] up against king Nebuchadnezzar. **(Daniel chapters 3 and 6).** The leaders must be moderate to paying attention to what people say about them and how people cheat them.

They're also to be careful with those who report others to them to discern the motivation of their reports. This does not imply that the leaders should be negligent over people comments and actions towards them. But the must be selective with they matters they should treat with strictness and those they should trivialise. If not some of the sycophant reporters will be misleading them (the leaders), causing them troubles and hatred against some other subjects who speak or act against them (the leaders). And the sycophants also causing punishing suffering from the leaders to such subjects.

*iv = **BEING STRICTLY LAWFUL** = (Prv 28:2, KJV).*

For the transgression of a land many are the princes thereof: But by a man of understanding and knowledge, the state thereof shall be prolonged.

= (Prov 25:4-5 NKJV) =

[4] Take away the dross from silver, And it will go to the silversmith for jewelry. [5] Take away the wicked from before the king, And his throne will be established in righteousness.

SUPPORTING TEXT = 2nd Tim 2:20-21.

Personal integrity is a crucial element in leadership. All leaders are known by all and are supported by some people for whom they the leaders are and what they do, whether the leaders are doing well or doing wrongly. This is because even when leaders are corrupt some people will still support them and benefit from their corrupt leadership, meanwhile those who hate corruption will be against the corrupt leaders and their corrupt leaderships. Yet the law of moderation by leadership demands that personal integrity must be appreciable to leaders and hence they should endeavour to shun corrupting their leadership but be fair in their leading, realising that their dignity is at stake in their leaderships and therefore attach their personal integrity to their various areas of leadership, and thereby exhibit true righteousness by moderate leadership. Corrupt advisors are so smart to getting close to and surround the leaders, yet the leaders with integrity are law abiding and they are persistent to ensure that the law of fairness is established and them being strict to taking the lead for obeying it while persuading all of their followers to do the same.

v = ESTABLISHING AND MAINTAINING JUSTICE = (Prv 16:10, NAS).

A divine decision is in the lips of the King, his mouth should not err in judgement .

= (Prv 29:4,14, NAS) =

The king gives stability to the land by justice, but a man who takes bribes overthrows it. 4. If a king judges the poor with truth, his throne will be established forever. V 14

Establishing justice in leadership is one of the elements of moderating personal conduct as a leader. It is therefore proper to be resolute to establishing and maintaining justice while pursuing righteousness through leadership. Justice is the basis for carrying everyone along in anything and justice in leadership is hereby the subject matter. There are those who hate fair leaders and their fair leadership, because the haters regard them as obstacles to their selfishness in the affairs of the people. But that is not a reason for the just leaders to begin to compromise, moreso because, any compromise deprives some people of their rights and privileges and discredit the integrity of the leaders and of their leadership, at the same time it's offensive to God.

*vi = **MENTORING WITH FAIRNESS IN LEADERSHIP** =*
(Prov 29:19,21, Amp).

[19] A servant will not be corrected by words alone; For though he understands, he will not respond [nor pay attention]. [21] He who pampers his slave from childhood Will find him to be a son in the end.

= (Prov29:19, 21 NASB2020) =

[19] A slave will not be instructed by words alone; For though he understands, there will be no response. [21] One who pampers his slave from childhood Will in the end find him to be rebellious.

Mentoring is also a part and parcel of the purposes of leaders.

Every leader must be a mentor or mentoress who is moderate to educating his subjects, because from the leader subjects mentoring successors and other patriotic citizens are produced. One of the reasons many leaders find it difficult to get the support of their followers for progressing their affairs is just because most of the followers are untrained and uninformed by their leaders who should be their dependable guides for knowing the right things to do and when to do them. The Christians are the greatest examples of the confused set of people under their own leaders who can't educate them well in regard to Christianity. Therefore: the Christian leaders must engage in training their church members with the accurate teachings of Jesus Christ, his modules operandi and of his purpose which we look up to for our functioning. Likewise: the religious and circular leaders are to be training their followers in the right way according to God's approval.

vii = MODERATING VISIONS, PLANS AND DECISIONS =
(Prv 16:2-3,33, AMP).

All the ways of a man are pure in his own eyes, but the Lord weighs the spirit (the thoughts and the intents of the heart). V 2. Roll your works upon the lord(commit and thrust them wholly to him; he will cause your thoughts to become agreeable to his will, and) so shall your plans be established and succeed. V 3. The lot is cast into the lap, but the decision is wholly of the lord(even the events that seem accidental are really ordered by him. V 33.

= (Prv 19:21, AMP) =

Many plans are in a man's mind, but it is the Lord's purpose for him that will stand.

= (Prv 29:18, AMP) =

Where there is no vision(no redemptive revelation of God) the people perish; but he who keeps the law(of God, which includes that, of man)-blessed(happy, fortunate, and enviable) is he.

SUPPORTING TEXTS =

1st Sam 16:7; Ps 33:10-11; Isa 46:26-27; Isa 46:10; Acts 5:39; Heb 12:4 Heb 617.

Because all humans are naturally imperfect; nobody is able to prospect, plans and make infallible decisions relating to his personal matters and the matters of his or her acquaintances, because definitely there are some determinant key factors to the results of the matter and the fates of the people in question.

Therefore it is wise and righteous to not only depend on self but to submit all self intelligence and confidence to God in the process of having foresight, planning and deciding for present and future matters. Further more; Many sins are committed through wrong, aspirations, plans and decisions and righteousness paradoxically is exhibited by aspiring, planning and deciding properly in accordance to God's principles and will about humans affairs.

There is no other ways true righteousness is displayed by having visions, planning and making decisions except the way of God. Even most visions, plans and decisions from circular governments, religions , labour forces, police, military and business entities for examples are not always in right standing with God; though the selfish interests for such visions, plans and decisions might be accomplished. Hence visions, plans and decisions must be moderate in the sense of permitting God's will and principle to guide and prevail over the visions, plans and decisions for that will help to perfect them and station the visionaries, planners and decision makers on the right track of executing righteousness by moderation of visions, plans and decisions. When all these are done everybody including God benefits from the visions, plans and decisions and will be happy with them, unless otherwise, the enthusiasts of evil will not be happy with them.

*viii = **FIGHTING INDISCIPLINE AND CORRUPTION =***
(Prov 25:4-5 NKJV).

[4] Take away the dross from silver, And it will go to the silversmith for jewelry. [5] Take away the wicked from before the king, And his throne will be established in righteousness.

= (Prov 20:26-27, NKJV) =

[26] A wise king sifts out the wicked, And brings the threshing wheel over them. [27] The spirit of a man is the lamp of the Lord, Searching all the inner depths of his heart.

Indiscipline and corruption is a characteristic cancer or any other terminal diseases in the humans body and their affairs. Indiscipline and corruption is the fundamental undoing of any government that permits it. There's an atom of it in every government around the world, but African governments are the worst, and the churches and religions are not exceptional. The general affairs of all of us humanity can never be truly prosperous in the midst of indiscipline and corruption especially while the governments set the pace for it. It's a necessity therefore: that the leaders of every class should be so resistant to all kinds of indiscipline, corruption and their perpetrators, to ensure the integrity of the communities is protect, knowing that it's the basis for a progressive prosperity.

MODERATING CONTENTION.

DEFINITION = Managing troublesome struggles with caution and discipline.

MEMORY VERSE = *Jms 3:16 AMP* =

For where jealousy and selfish ambition exist, there is disorder [unrest, rebellion] and every evil thing and morally degrading practice.

INTRODUCTION

Contention is one of the phenomenons nobody can just stop from erupting, even though some of us can control ourselves so we should not be the causes of the contention, yet we cannot really control every other person to be like us. One striking factor for this reality is that some people believe in prospering by pacifism while some believe in prospering by contention. Some believe in prosperity by legitimacy while some believe in prosperity by illegitimacy. Some believe in prospering by honesty while some believe in prospering by lies. Some trust in their integrity while some trust in their compromise. Some believe in discipline while others believe in corruption. Some believe in God, some believe in Santa. Private citizens and governments make up the peoples in question. For the continual existence of this fact contention can never cease among us in this world. The higher powerful nations of the world have being in an age long struggle to calm national and international contentions and to establish peace in replacement of them, but never have they truly achieved it. I can assure the world that every humans effort to eradicating contention and establishing world peace is an impossible mission, my reason being that almost all of those masterminding the global treaty are the cause of the contentions and are never really serious to end them due to their selfish investments in the contentions. This lesson is about learning how to deal with contentions and never be overwhelmed by them but defeating them with some strategic wisdoms.

---

i = REFRAINING FROM CONTENTION = (Prv 17:14, KJV).

The beginning of strife is as when one leteth out water; Therefore leave out contention before it will be meddled.

(Prov 14:16, AMP)

A wise man suspects danger and cautiously avoids evil, But the fool is arrogant and careless.

Though we are offended many at times, we have the obligation of refraining from contentions because that's one way of avoiding being more grieved by the offenders and through dwelling in the contention we revenge on them. Our vengeance should always be executed as last or never an option for self defence against oppressions, meanwhile; as we have the option of despising trivial offenses and refraining from contentions since we are not immensely hurt through them: we should do so, not as resulted from our weaknesses and cowardice, but to honour God by handing our vengeance over to him, and for the righteous reason of moderating our ways of vengeance. So to be in right standing with God through this aspect of life we are to find every reason to force ourselves to not participate in and to avoid contentions.

> *ii = **RELYING ON GOD'S VENGEANCE** =*
> *(Prv 17:13; Prv 20:22, KJV).*

> *Whoso rewardeth evil for good, Evil shall not depart from his house. :13.*

> *Say thou not I will recompense evil : but wait on the Lord and he shall save thee. :22.*

> **SUPPORTING TEXTS =**

> **2nd Sam 16:12; Rom 12:17-21; 1st Thes 5:15; 1st Pet 3:9 .**

We can discover that in most cases when we do good to some people they eventually do not appreciate the good we do to them; and they rather reward us with evil for the good we have done to the. And in some ways we reward others with evil for some sorts of goodness we benefit from them. However the cases may be, no one should rely on self revenge in the process of pursuing righteousness of moderation but the moderation venturer must rely on God to avenge for the evil paid to him for good by others , while he or she repents and diligently refrain from ungratefulness and paying back evil for good. Nobody will really be comfortable if each of us is to take revenge for the evil he or she receives from others whom he or she's good to, because all of us can be good and all of us can be evil since each of us pay with evil for good.

iii = *KINDLY FEEDING THE HUNGRY ADVERSARIES =*
(Prv 25:21,22, KJV).

If thine enemy be hungry, give him bread to eat; if he be thirsty, give him water to drink. 21. For thou shalt heap coals of fire upon up on his head, and the Lord shall reward thee. V 22.

Feeding the hungry adversary is one of the ways of showing love to the enemies. It's true that many humans cannot have the fortitude to tolerate grievous insolency, assaults and some sorts of witchcraft attitudes, and thereby the offended become eager to regularly avenge on the offenders. But in the case of pursuing contentment by moderation. There is an obligation to exercise fortitude towards the ignorant and unwilling offenders, or the willing offenders, not because of personal weakness of the offended but because of the consideration that we are to be constant in relating wisely with God, and that he is permanently able as he promises to avenge perfectly upon our adversaries more than we can do on our own. And that for depending on God in dealing with the adversaries, God never leaves us unrewarded but definitely decorates our lives and situations with his own desired progress, prosperity and success.

*iv = **FORBIDDING TO OVER CELEBRATE THE FALL OF THE
ADVERSARIES = (Prv 24:17-18, KJV).***

*Rejoice not when thy enemy falleth, and let not thine heart
be glad when he stumbleth. V 17. Lest the Lord see it, and it
displeaseth him, and he turn away his wrath from him. V 18.*

Over celebrating the fall of the adversaries is a sin, because
we are to be conscious of whatever we do and not to do it
excessively so not to sin true excess behaviours. Having excess
celebration over the fall of the enemies is to be forbidden in the
race to attaining contentment through moderation. Hence we
are to not indulge in celebrating the fall of our enemies but our
God given victory over the adversaries should be the rightful
reason for us to celebrate when our enemies are suffering
from their dooms. Nevertheless: the celebration should not
go beyond expression of joy to becoming a mockery to the
defeated foes. This should be done because over celebrating
the fall of the enemies is a means of avenging on them but
pitying them for their dooms while rejoicing and glorifying God
for our victory is a justified evidence of exhibiting contentment
by moderating vengeance. We must have in mind that God can
turn around the groaning of our foes for their comfortable
recovery when we over celebrate their fall in jesting.

*v = **AVOIDING JEALOUSY** = (James 4:1-3 AMP).*

*[1] What leads to [the unending] quarrels and conflicts
among you? Do they not come from your [hedonistic] desires
that wage war in your [bodily] members [fighting for control
over you]? [2] You are jealous and covet [what others have]
and your lust goes unfulfilled; so you murder. You are envious
and cannot obtain [the object of your envy]; so you fight and*

battle. You do not have because you do not ask [it of God]. [1 John 3:15] [3] You ask [God for something] and do not receive it, because you ask with wrong motives [out of selfishness or with an unrighteous agenda], so that [when you get what you want] you may spend it on your [hedonistic] desires.

Jealousy from the mind triggers antagonistic and intimidating reactions to people who are outperforming the jealous. The jealous want to earn the highest credit and glory including prosperity. They love being on the top and being in control and are furious to destroy whatever they cannot bring under their control. This further means they have the mindset of whatever they will not be in charge of no other person will be in charge of it. I don't mean only the jealous are leaders or are in control but they're happy to have other leaders or controllers as their subordinates but they are never submissive to any superior to them. They agree to be subordinates only because they have no option, but at any slightest opportunity they step up for surpassing by legitimacy of usurping their superiors. But they can really be submissive and subordinate only if they can remove jealousy in their heart and life and free their mind to live and serve within their due means and statuses. We all are responsible to remove our own jealousy in whichever way we express it.

vi = LIVING IN THE WISDOM OF GOD = (Jms 3:13-18, AMP).

[13] Who among you is wise and intelligent? Let him by his good conduct show his [good] deeds with the gentleness and humility of true wisdom. [14] But if you have bitter jealousy and selfish ambition in your hearts, do not be arrogant, and [as a result] be in defiance of the truth. [15] This [superficial]

wisdom is not that which comes down from above, but is earthly (secular), natural (unspiritual), even demonic. [16] For where jealousy and selfish ambition exist, there is disorder [unrest, rebellion] and every evil thing and morally degrading practice. [17] But the wisdom from above is first pure [morally and spiritually undefiled], then peace-loving [courteous, considerate], gentle, reasonable [and willing to listen], full of compassion and good fruits. It is unwavering, without [self-righteous] hypocrisy [and self-serving guile]. [18] And the seed whose fruit is righteousness (spiritual maturity) is sown in peace by those who make peace [by actively encouraging goodwill between individuals].

Jealousy and envy in addition to the contention they bring are some of the manifestations of living in Human wisdom. Selfishness, rebellion and lust which bring them are some other aspects of living in carnal wisdom, and contention is the utmost result of it. But we can conquer the contention and live contentedly only if we can adapt to living in the wisdom of God which replaces our human nature and mindset with godly nature and mindset. And by then we can be able to drop our lustful purpose for God's lovely purpose in all of our dealings.

Chapter 14

BEING TEACHABLE THAN BEING SCORNFUL

DEFINITION = 1 = Having a submissive attitude for learning.

2 = Being willing and open to learning, and not making jest of teachings and whoever that teaches.

3 = Being rationally reasonable rather than being conceited, opinionated and arrogant.

MEMORY VERSES = *Prov 14:9 AMP = Fools mock sin [but sin mocks the fools], But among the upright there is good will and the Favour and blessing of God. [Prov 10:23]*

> *Prov = 15:12 AMP = A scoffer [unlike a wise man] resents one who rebukes him and tries to teach him; Nor will he go to the wise [for counsel and instruction].*

INTRODUCTION

Have you ever noticed that there is always disagreement and controversy among people just because of how they react to stated facts, fictions, truths, lies, realities, falsehoods, debunking and corrections.

All of the listed factors are components of education, the two basic conflicting factors of teaching and learning are reality and falsehood. Whatever that is taught is either real or false. Whatever anybody says is either real or false. So controversy and contention is inevitable as long as reality and falsehood are available in any saying or teaching. However I'm focusing on revealing the fact that there is also discrepancy, controversy and contention in the situation where only real sayings and teachings is available. The reason is that there are people who hate to face the reality and accept it as far as it counters what ever they say, believe or want, while there are people who not only acknowledge the reality by accepting it but go further to inform others with it. Two sets of disagreeing people cannot work together (collaborate, cooperate). There has being a battle of the mind and of learning in the life of humans caused by God and satan starting from the time of Eve and Adam. God taught Adam and Eve that they and their glory should die if they should rebel against him, but they should continue to live as long as they continue to obey him. But Satan counter- taught them that, they should not die if they should rebel against God. So they got distracted and confused over the both conflicting teachings, then they preferred Satan's teaching to rebelling against God. Therefore their glorious life and opportunities and privileges died even when they were still living in the physical. But Jesus Christ came to be tested with the same conflicting teachings and he preferred God's own teaching to obeying him and sustained his glorious life and opportunities, setting the pace of living a contented life in the aspect of moderate learning. Jesus by his attitudinal learning demonstrates we should be strictly selective with what we learn and we are to learn only the real things which align with what God teaches.

---

i = SHUNNING SELF CONCEIT AND BEING RIGHTLY TEACHABLE = (Prv 3:5-7, AMP).

Lean on, trust in and be confident in the Lord with all your heart and mind and do not rely on your own Insight or understanding. V 5. In all your ways, know, recognise and acknowledge him, and he will direct and make straight and plain your paths. V 6. Be not wise in your own eyes, reverently fear and worship the Lord and turn(entirely)from evil. 7.

All of humans without the knowledge, the understanding and the wisdom from God are conceited in the sense that they're living with their mediocre, knowledge, understanding and wisdom and are not humble to learn from God. But those who have humbled themselves to learning from God and are living by his way of knowledge, understanding and wisdom are contented in their mind, spirit and souls in contrast to the conceited people who have shattered mind, shattered spirit and shattered souls. The reason the majority of the world population is regularly frustrated and upset is just because they're conceited and never want to learn from God. But the very few who surrender their own intelligence to learn from God all around the world are satisfied within themselves. God has the infallible education and the whole world should live in excellence if all of us conform to God's education and authority.

*ii = **DEFEATING IMPULSIVE RESPONSES WITH MEDITATED***
   RESPONSES = (Prv 18:13, AMP).

He who answers a matter before he hears the fact _ it is folly
and shame to him.

It's so rampant for people to be fooling and shaming themselves by being so quick to interject and interrupt to respond to anyone talking to them or talking to a group of people which he the interjector belongs. Some of the interjecting responders do so because they believe they know it all, believing that the remaining part of whatever the speakers intend to say are no more needed, and having the motive of subduing all other views and opinions to influence the people with their own views and opinions so to seem to be superior, but only for them to realise they have missed the point and the contextual matters of the talks when their impulsive responses are truly debunked. It is imperative then that we all learn how to be selfless, patient in discussions and to premeditate on each of the response we should give. Doing this helps us moderate our responses, protect our dignity of talking habitat, prevents us from self fooling and shaming, making people to respect us for giving reasonable responses and to consider our natural and unintentional flaws when we mistake in responding.

*iii = **CONFORMING TO WISE MENTORS = (Prv 22:17-19, AMP).***

Listen (consent and submit)to the words of the wise, and
apply your mind to my knowledge. V 17. For it will be pleasant
if you keep them in your mind (believing them); your lips will
be accustomed to (confessing) them. V 18.. So that your
trust(believe, reliance, support, and confidence) may be I
the Lord, I have made known these things to you today, even
to you. V 19.

One of the way forward to learning and increasing in learning is to recognise the value of mentoring and of the mentors. However we shouldn't fail to reflect on the fact that there are good mentors with good mentorship and there are bad mentors with bad mentorship. So we should be careful with the kinds of mentors and mentoring we value and receive. Most people are corrupted with bad mentoring by the bad mentors while the few of us are trained to be virtuous with good mentoring by the good mentors. The good and bad of this matter are available and operational in the churches, the religious centres, the streets and academic / vocational centres. So to moderate one's learning manner in relating with the mentors, he or she is responsible for identifying the good mentors and to be humbly learning from them, and to jettison every bad mentor so to free himself/herself from the problems bad mentors and bad mentoring develop in people's mind and lives. All of good mentors are God's representative educators on earth. But all of bad mentors are Satan's representative educators also here on earth. It's then in our will power, choice and decision to obediently be relating with good mentors and mentoresses and to be learning from every good instruction they can afford.

iv = SUBMITTING TO CHASTISEMENT = (Prov 23:12 AMP).

Apply your heart to discipline And your ears to words of knowledge.

All of us humans have our areas of flaws which make us imperfect. Therefore we all are liable to misbehaving in different ways, and all of us will become reprobates if there is no corrective measures for redirecting us. However: there are reprobate people among whom some have no corrections given them and those who intentionally reject corrections to continue with their erroneous ways. But to moderate and improve our behaviours we must be receptive to chastisement which is not meant to destroy us but to discipline us from misbehaving and for us to retrace our steps from the wrong paths, bringing them back to the right path of Life which is certainly God and his own way.

v = LIVING IN GODLY WISDOM = (Prv 26:12, AMP).

Do you see a man wise in his own eyes and conceit? There is more hope for a(self confident)fool than for him.

= (Prv 28:26, AMP) =

He who lean on, trust in, and is self confident of his own mind and heart is a (self confident) fool but he who walks in skillful and godly wisdom shall be delivered.

SUPPORTING TEXTS.

Luke 18:11-14; John 7:50-51; Rom 12:16; Jms 1:5; Rev 3:17-19 .

Self conceit is like a sinful attitude that gives birth to its self conceited children which are for examples: over carnal confidence, arrogance and unteachachability. Self conceit encourages its victims to remain ignorant concerning some significant insights they should acquire to augment their personal behaviours and living standards, making them sinners therein. Nevertheless those who truly desire to live righteously by moderating learning should not only be teachable to rightful circular teachings and circular mentors, the seekers of righteousness and contentment by moderating learning attitudes must be likewise teachable to God, by endeavouring to obey his laws and precepts and the real God anointed mentors. It's not easy to surrender to the wisdom of God and to be learning from it, unless there is the recognition of the supremacy of his wisdom and the willingness to jettison our lusts and our own wisdom for fulfilling them. We are also to acknowledge the fact that, self conceit and carnal wisdom lead their exhibitionists into frustration and hopelessness, but godly conception and wisdom lead their conformists to true prosperity and hopefulness.

*vi = **SHUNNING SENTIMENTS AND ADAPTING TO THE FACTS** = (Prv 23:23, AMP).*

Buy the truth and sell it not; not only that, but also get discernment and judgement, instruction and understanding.

Some people delight in sentimental words that vindicate their selfish acts and desires, while they the sentimental hearers keep on missing the realities of life and all that surround life; due to their hate and resistance to adopting the truth. However; nobody's sentiments have the capacity to alter the facts in all ramifications of life. So this simply justifies the biblical statement apostle Paul makes: saying, we can do nothing against the truth but for the truth.

= (2nd Cor 13:7-8 AMP) =

[7] But I pray to God that you may do nothing wrong. Not so that we [and our teaching] may appear to be approved, but that you may continue doing what is right, even though we

[by comparison] may seem to have failed. [8] For we can do nothing against the truth, but only for the truth [and the gospel—the good news of salvation].

Meaning furthermore that righteousness is approved by promoting the factual truths and not fighting against it by all manners. For doing that is a sin of sentimental acceptance of the truth which is founded upon impacable God's word, and the truth is not authentic when sentiments are attached to it. So the truth must remain the factual impacable word of God according to the facts from the bible and proclaimed by many sincere gospel and circular witnesses. Therefore; moderating learning in the endeavour to pursuing contentment: demands acknowledging and submitting to the truth, to be totally free from the guilt of obstinacy, reprobation and unrepentance, as we know that we shall know the truth while the truth we know and comply to redeems us from guilts and obscurities of various sorts.

vii = **DEFEATING CREDULITY WITH DISCRETION IN LEARNING = (Prv 23:23, AMP)**

Buy the truth and sell it not; not only that, but also get discernment and judgement, instruction and understanding.

= (Prov 14:15, AMP) =

The naive or inexperienced person [is easily misled and] believes every word he hears, But the prudent man [is discreet and astute and] considers well where he is going.

Many people commit sin through credulity, because they have the task of verifying various informations, teaching, preaching, prophecies, counselling, all kinds of religious, academic and social education they receive from people; regardless of social or religious status of their mentors. Because many miserable conditions tormenting people in diverse ways result from their credulity which leads its victims to consistently wallowing in perplexity and intensified ignorance, and thereby eventually commit the sins of doing the wrong things for not knowing the right things which has being the cause of their tragedy. But discretion and inquisition in learning help to provide the learners with some clarifications and certainties, and at times the inquisition in learning exposes the fallacies of the fake and mediocre mentors, and the discrete proteges / mentees hence amend their adoption to the mentorship they are given. While doing that; the discrete learners begin moderating their beliefs of learning in other not to fault through falsified knowledge and its applications. But ensuring that they diligently receive, comply to and apply the authentic informations and education offered to them.

Chapter 15

MODERATING DRESSING.

DEFINITION = Moderating dressing is wearing clothes and other fashion and vocation accessories in modest ways.

INTRODUCTION

Clothing and wearing of all fashion and attires are not without purposes. One major purpose of dressing is to serve the purposes for which it is made. Some clothing methods are not more than to serve as mere fashions; some of dressing modes are worn by distinct civil businesses and vocational groups and organisations as their various uniform for identifications.

Even most religious and traditional officials with the inclusion of all aristocrats also wear their patterns of identity fashions.

There are also other kinds of dressing people wear to serve their various ungodly and lustful interests . Some examples are most young and adult females or males who dress sexually attractive to entice the Young and old opposite genders and lure them into sexually immorality, through adultery, fornication, incest and many more ways of sexual sins. There are other sets of people who wear fashions not to get involved in sexual sins, yet they sin by dressing for showing off, which emanate from their ungodly prides. While some people hate dressing pompously and delight in simplicity and decency of the highest order concerning their dressing methods both in their different religious circles and in in the circular environments.

Whichever ways: the prior essences of this lesson are to remind us of the relevance and irrelevance of our dressing styles for they either promote good virtues and godliness in us or our lack of good virtues and godlessness. Though the singular climax factor of bodily clothing and wearing of foot wears are for properly covering bodily nakedness and protection from bruises and cuts on the foot. We should not always forget that our righteousness and unrighteousness, our moderation to contentment and our immoderation and discontentment are also measured with our dressing modes. So then it is important we refrain from all sorts of dressing which are not in accordance with God's own will and purposes. Because as God judges all other affairs of ours he also judges our dressing life, and justifies or condemns them when he measures the said about our dressing life on the scales of his pleasure and displeasure, as we understand that respite that righteousness can be justified in all other aspects of life, yet ungodly dressing alone can disqualify its enthusiasts from relating perfectly with God and entering into God's Kingdom of glory. So we should always moderate our dressing to please God therewith so to please God and partake from all of his blessings.

i = DRESSING ACCORDING TO GENDERS = (Deut 22:5, KJV).

The woman shall not wear that which pertaineth unto a man, neither shall a man put on a woman's garment: for all that do so are abomination unto the Lord thy God.

= (1st Tim 2:9-10 NKJV) =

[9] in like manner also, that the women adorn themselves in modest apparel, with propriety and moderation, not with braided hair or gold or pearls or costly clothing, [10] but, which is proper for women professing godliness, with good works.

Godliness is expected in term of dressing, it is important we realise that God is not insensitive in creating humans in two opposite genders. We should rather understand that God has his perfect purposes for the two genders creation of humanity, and that God's own purposes for It stand supreme. Henceforth; all humans are commanded by God through his written scripture that we should observe the law of properly distinctive genders dressing, as our various routine fashions, occupational uniforms and religious fashions. Our individuals and collective efforts to observing the God commanded genders dressing proffer our delightment in moderation and contentment through proper dressing.

However; many different peoples strive to undermine the gravity of the divine demand for proper dressings among males and females, by dressing according to their various personal and groups pleasures which contradict God's own pleasure pertaining to wearing of fashions. Also those who forsake God's righteousness for their own righteousness concerning dressing, always endeavour to defend and justify their ungodliness by dressing through their proposition of divers logics and self justification against the reality of the gospel and the will of God about dressing.

Nevertheless the word and the will of God stand sure, and God is not a respecter of any person by being sentimental. Therefore it is either that God's will and purposes are fulfilled or they are abandoned in our various genders dressing at any given time. Some of the logics people propose concerning genders dressing modes are that; if the bibles means that women shouldn't wear trousers while men shouldn't wear neither gowns nor skirts and blouses, as it is popularly conceived that trousers always belong to males, while skirts, blouses and gowns, including tying of wrappers belong to women.

Yet to the knowledge of very few among people's of contemporary generations, no singular and collective sets of people ever have wearing of trousers of any design by female as part of their cultures with the exception of the Indians, parkistanis and some other Arab nations whose females dress in their bogus traditional trousers. The Scottish men of the olden times have a traditional wearing of skirts.

Moreso no human traditions, logic or self will defy God's own tradition, will and facts, as using dressing matters as cases examples. So we should always try to understand the ways and will of God in all we do as that should be evident in our dressing. So we should consistently desert our personal will and let the will of God stand through our dressing.

I cannot conclude that God will not allow the women who have this knowledge yet choose to be wearing trousers into his heavenly kingdom because of it. I cannot also conclude that those Scottish men who wear skirts will go to hell for it. But I can conclude that if the women wearers of trousers and men wearers of skirts intentionally do so to tempt God they will go to hell for it if they can't repent on time. But those who wear them with innocent intentions may be permitted into God's heavenly Kingdom.

ii = WEARING GARMENTS OF MORAL PURITY = (Eccl 9:8, AMP).

Let your garment be always white(with purity), and let your head not lack (the) oil (of gladness).

= (1st Peter 3:1-12 NKJ) =

[1] Wives, likewise, be submissive to your own husbands, that even if some do not obey the word, they, without a word, may be won by the conduct of their wives, [2] when they observe your chaste conduct accompanied by fear. [3] Do not let your adornment be merely outward—arranging the hair, wearing gold, or putting on fine apparel— [4] rather let it be the hidden person of the heart, with the incorruptible beauty of a gentle and quiet spirit, which is very precious in the sight of God. [5] For in this manner, in former times, the holy women who trusted in God also adorned themselves, being submissive to their own husbands, [6] as Sarah obeyed Abraham, calling him lord, whose daughters you are if you do good and are not afraid with any terror. [7] Husbands, likewise, dwell with them with understanding, giving honour to the wife, as to the weaker vessel, and as being heirs together of the grace of life, that your prayers may not be hindered. [8] Finally, all of you be of one mind, having compassion for one another; love as brothers, be

tenderhearted, be courteous; [9] not returning evil for evil or reviling for reviling, but on the contrary blessing, knowing that you were called to this, that you may inherit a blessing. [10] For "He who would love life And see good days, Let him refrain his tongue from evil, And his lips from speaking deceit. [11] Let him turn away from evil and do good; Let him seek peace and pursue it. [12] For the eyes of the Lord are on the righteous, And His ears are open to their prayers; But the face of the Lord is against those who do evil."

= (1st Tim 6:9-10, AMP) =

Also (I desire) that women should adorn themselves, modestly and appropriately and sensibly in seemingly apparel, not with (elaborate) hair arrangement or gold or pearl or expensive clothing . V 9 . But by doing good deeds (deeds in themselves good and for the good and advantage of those contacted by them) , as befits women who profess reverential fear for and devotion to God. V 10.

We are hereby admonished to always wear both internal and external righteousness as our fashions lifestyles. The both humanly genders are responsible to exhibit God approved righteousness though displaying of good morality in all ramifications of life. Hence godliness takes the centre stages Just as it is obvious from the texts that women are advised to wear the garments of true submission to their various husbands, while resenting ostentatious outward dressing, also that the women should guide the young females to follow suit in being submissive and living in general godliness.

Adult men are also persuaded to always show true love to their wives first, then to others and they the men should wear the garment of moral righteousness at all times and teach their younger ones to do the same, knowing that though we as humans may please God through our physical fashions yet we can err through the moral aspects of fashions if we fail to live up to God's expectation for it.

Good morality should be sequent to bodily decent fashioning in the divine law of moderate dressing.

ESV = Ps 132:9; Isaiah 59:17; Isaiah 61:10; Isaiah 11:5; Ephesians 6:14; 1 Thessalonians 5:8

= (Ps 132:9: 9) =

Let your priests' be clothed with righteousness, And let your saints shout for joy.

= (Isah 59:17) =

He put on righteousness as a breastplate, And a helmet of salvation on his head; He put on garments of vengeance for clothing, And wrapped himself in zeal as a cloak.

= (Isah 61:10) =

I will greatly rejoice in the Lord; My soul shall exult in my God, for he has clothed me with the garments of salvation; He has covered me with the robe of righteousness, As a bridegroom decks himself like a priest with a beautiful headdress, and as a bride adorns herself with her jewels.

= (Isah 11:5) =

Righteousness shall be the belt of his waist, And faithfulness the belt of his loins.

= (Eph 6:14) =

Stand therefore, having fastened on the belt of truth, and shaving put on the breastplate of righteousness.

= (1st Thes 5:8) =

But since we belong to the day, let us be sober, having put on the breastplate of faith and love, and for a helmet the hope of salvation.

God speaking through many of his servants requires all of us to wear Righteousness as garments. This means Righteousness is to be our character and personality in every respect and it indicate the restoration of God's image and kingdom in our body, soul, spirit and entire life.

iii = *ESCHEWING OSTENTATION AND DRESSING HUMBLY =*
(Isah 3:16-26, NAS).

Moreover the Lord said, because the daughters of zion are proud, and walk with heads held high, and seductive eyes, and go along with mincing steps and tinkle the angles on their feet. 16. Therefore the Lord will afflict the scalp of the daughters of zion with scabs, and the Lord will make their forehead bare. V 17. In that day the Lord will take away the beauty of heir anklets, head bands crescent ornaments V 18. Dangling earrings, bracelets or chains, and the spangle face veils and scarfs. V 19. Headdresses, ankle chains, sashes, perfume boxes, amulets. 20. Finger rings, nose rings. V 21. Festal robes, outer tunics, cloaks, money purses. V 22. Hand mirrors, undergarments, turbans and veils. V 23. Now it will come about, that instead of sweet perfume there will be putrefaction: instead of a belt a rope, instead of well set hair a plucked out scalp; instead of clothe, a donning of sackcloth; and branding instead of beauty. V 24. Your men will fall by the sword and your mighty Ones in battle. V 25. And her gates will lament and mourn, and deserted she will sit on the ground. V 26.

= (1st Tim 2:9-10, AMP) =

Also (I desire) that women should adorn themselves modestly and appropriately and sensibly in seemingly apparel, not with (elaborate) hair arrangement or gold or pearls or expensive clothing . V 9. But by doing good deeds (deeds in themselves good and for the good and advantage of those contacted by them) , as befits women who profess reverential fear for and devotion to God. V 10.

Dressing and fashioning generally are Purposed to exhibit decency of personality As it should be evident in the bodily decency of dressing and not for ungodly pride and ostentation. So wearing of fashions of all kinds must not be for the essence of showing off, as we know that pride and ostentation are sins and displaying pride and ostentation in dressing is not exempted from sin. Hence dressing must be moderate through eliminating fashioning pride and ostentation while constantly dressing in decent manners to show personal humility to God. Because immoral pride and ostentation are not From God but they are products of human nature and demons of worldliness. The holy spirit is not in tune with a pompous heart, so the pompous heart of ostentatious dressing does not connect with the holy spirit to worship God in the spirit and the truth. For us to be Spiritually tuned for sweet fellowship with God ostentation which is exemplified with prideful dressing must be removed from our inside out.

iv = *SHUNNING ANXIETY ABOUT DRESSING* =
(Matt 6:28-34, AMP)

And why should you be anxious about clothes? Consider the Lilies of the field and learn thoroughly how they grow; they neither toil nor spin. V 28. Yet I tell you, even Solomon, in all his magnificence(excellence, dignity and grace) was not arrayed like one of these. V 29. But if God so clothe the grass of the field, which today is alive, and tomorrow tossed into the furnace, will he not much more clothe you, o you of little faith. V 30. Therefore do not worry and be anxious, saying, what are we going to have and eat? Or what are we going to have to drink? Or what are we going to have to wear? For the gentiles (heathen) wish for and crave and diligently seek all these things, and your heavenly father knows well that you them all. V 32. But seek (aim at and strive after) first of all his Kingdom and his righteousness(his way of doing and being right), and then shall all these things taken together will be given you besides. V 33. So do not worry and be anxious about tomorrow, for tomorrow will have worries and anxieties of its own, sufficient for each day is its own trouble. V 34.

SUPPORTING TEXT = 1 Kgs 10:4-7.

Anxiety is one of the major deficiency of Man that consistently sets man's foot on the path of enticements and temptations. And when people are victims of anxiety they are liable to become desperate towards meeting their diverse selfish desires. There is nothing wrong about desiring to be clothed but being anxious with dressing up is wrong and sinful. So we should be moderate in our desiring to get what we should wear, by not being anxious and desperate for clothing ourselves, but our major concern should be to live in God's righteousness continually while we engage in our personal means of livelihoods, while believing that God will prosper our genuine occupations and that from our incomes and God's miraculous providence we should have some money and humans favour with which we can get our necessary wears.

Also we should not be competing with others in fashioning through anxiety and desperation as generated from pressure for how we should be resented by others if we don't meet their expected standard of dressing for us. Rather we should prioritise the divine purposes of wearing fashions. Therefore we should please God by observing his own purposes for wearing clothes and fashion and not pleasing humans by being anxiously and desperately to meet the ungodly standard that the world set for us about wearing clothes and fashions. It's better that God approves our dressings and we live in peace with him than for us to win against him and live in enmity with him in the attempt to please ourselves and the world in clothing.

v = DRESSING FOR PRIESTLEY SERVICE = (Exd 28:1-2, KJV).

And take thou thee Aaron thy brother, and his sons with him, from among the children of Israel, that he may minister to me in the priest's office , even Aaron, Nadab and Abihu, Eliazer and Ithamar, Aaron's sons. V 1. And thou shalt make holy garments for Aaron thy brother for glory and for beauty. V 2.

= (Exd 29:5-9,29, KJV) =

And thou shalt take the garment, and put upon Aaron the coat and the robe of ephod, and the ephod and the breastplate, and gird him with the curious girdle of the ephod. V 5. And thou shalt put the mitre upon his head and put the holy crown upon the mitre. V 6. Then thou shalt take the anointing oil, and pour it upon his head, and anoint him. V 7. And thou shalt bring his sons and put coats upon them. V 8. And thou shalt gird them with girdle, and Aaron and his sons, and put the bonnets on them: and the priest's office shall be theirs for a special statute: and thou shalt consecrate Aaron and his sons. V 9. And the holy garments of Aaron shall be his sins' after him, to be anointed therein and to be consecrated in them. V 29.

= (Exd 31:10, KJV) =

And the clothes of service, and the holy garments for Aaron the priest, and the garments of his sons to minister in the priest's office.

= (Exd 39:1, KJV) =

And of the blue, the purple, and scarlet, they made clothes of service to do service in the holy place, and made the holy garments, for Aaron as the Lord commanded Moses.

Dressing in official attires is part of religious life: and dressing in theological official clothes and fashion accessories is the emphatic example of dressing in religious attires. From the contents of the texts, it is observed that God wills to dress his servants which the theological priests exemplify; sacredly, elegantly and splendidly. The three distinct factors as seen in the God instituted dressing appearance of his servant priests portray the few among many specialities pertaining to godly dressing and that all of the specialities are meant to teach us holiness, inheriting honour and glory in the Lord. We are also to learn from here that holiness, splendours and glory are meant to be few among much more identities of peculiarities for the God's people starting from the priests and downward, but though the priests are committed with distinction of God given mandates while other lower classes of people among the church have their various functions. In all the examples as stated are to lead us in the path of moderating our dressing as people of God: as we know that we are royal priesthood a holy Godly nation who are called and redeemed from the darkness of worldliness of which ungodly dressing is an example; to lighten the physical earthly environments with true godliness, using godly and decent dressing as a case study, and forbidding all kinds of ungodly dressing appearances as God's own sons and daughters. We are to perfectly represent God in our dressing modules.

vi = *PRIESTLY ATTIRES SHOULD BE TRANS GENERATIONAL =* (Exd 29:9,29, KJV).

And thou shalt gird them with girdle, Aaron and his son, and put the bonnets on him: and the priest's office shall be theirs for a perpetual statutes: and thou shalt consecrate Aaron and his sons. V 9. And the holy garments of Aaron shall be his sons' after him, to be anointed therein and to be consecrated in them.

= (Num 20:23-28, KJV) =

And the Lord spake unto Moses and Aaron in mount hor, by the coast of the land of Edom, saying, V 23. Aaron shall be gathered unto his people: for he shall not enter into the land which I have given unto the children of Israel, because ye rebelled against my word in the water of Meribah. V 24. Take Aaron and his sons and bring them up in the mount Hor. V 25.

And strip Aaron of his garments, and put them upon Eleazer his son ! And Aaron shall be gathered unto his people, and shall die there. V 26. And Moses did as the Lord said, and they went into mount Hor in the sight of all congregation. V 27. And Moses stripped Aaron of his garments, and put them upon Eleazer his son: and Aaron died there on the top of the mount: and Moses and Eleazer came down from the mount. V 28.

We are to learn from the text that there is the need to transfer true and noble godly attires and dressing styles from parents to children. To extend the explanation on this segment of learning is to say we should understand that Christian parents and mentors generally are under obligation to teach their children on how they must dress to fulfill God's pleasure and purposes in their theological life, the parents and mentors must do that so they won't permit their children to be exposed to worldliness and more especially worldly dressing and that their children should learn to moderate their dressing by avoiding worldly dressing which they will learn out from the church when they are exposed to the world's systems. All these must be done to establish righteousness by dressing from parents/mentors to children/proteges and from the children/proteges to God's justification on contentment by moderate dressing. This systematic dressing is to be transferred from generation to generation.

vi = *PRIESTLEY DRESSING NOT A GUARANTEE FOR JUSTIFICATION = (Ezek 44:10,17,KJV).*

And the Levites that are gone away far from me , when Israel went astray away from me alter their idols; they shall bear their iniquity. V 10. And it shall come to pass that when they enter at the gates of their inner courts, and within. V 17. They shall have inner bonnets upon their heads, and shall have linen breeches upon their loins; they shall not gird themselves with anything that causeth sweat. V 18.

SUPPOTING TEXTS = Exd 28:40; Exd 29:9; Lev 8:5-15;

Though we may dress outwardly elegant as God's people yet, that is not all that God requires for perfect righteousness. So the righteousness derived from moderate dressing is just one element of righteousness and righteousness from all other aspects of life are required. As the word of God reveals that whosoever obeys the whole of God's laws and offend in one has failed in all of them, likewise whoever observes only outward righteousness and fails to observe habitual righteousness has failed in all of the law of righteousness.

= (James 2:10, NKJV) =

For whoever shall keep the whole law, and yet stumble in one point, he is guilty of all.

Righteous by dressing is therefore to be moderated through external modest dressing in link with the internal modest dressing which is obvious in true godly virtues.

vii = AS ARISTOCRATIC DRESSING = (Ps 45:13-14, KJV).

The King's daughter is all glorious within, her clothing is of wrought gold. V 13. She shall be brought unto the king in raiment of needlework: the virgins, her companions that follow her shall be brought unto thee. V 14.

= (Acts 12:21, KJV) =

And upon a set day, Herod arrayed in a royal apparel sat upon the throne, and made an oration unto them.

It is hereby brought to our comprehension that, as circular the princes and Princess are peculiarly identified with their aristocratic dressing so the church who are the princes and Princesses of the supremely theocratic Kingdom should be identified in special ways through their special clerical and general theological dressing patterns. We are also to demarcate between worldly aristocrats and their dressing methods from the theocratic aristocrats and our own dressing methods. Thereafter; the theocratic princess and princesses should not dare indulge in dressing like the ungodly princess and princesses because the circular royal traditional attires don't always link to God required theocratic moderate dressing. Though the circular royal traditional attires at times do not contradict God's righteousness, yet we the God's own must ensure that all of our dressing modes should be in exact to Godly modest dressing, which present the church prestigious in the world societies and glorifying to God therein. Because living a life of separation from the world is a pivotal part of Christianity, and dressing separately honourable to God's glory from circular traditional dressing that do not glorify the almighty God is to be taking seriously among the church. Righteousness and contentment through moderate dressing is accomplish by doing so.

*viii = **DRESSING AS TRADITIONAL ROYAL OFFICIALS =***
(Esth 8:15, KJV).

And Mordecai went out of the presence of the King in royal apparel of blue and white , and with a great crown of glory, and with a garment of fine linen and purple: and the city of shush an rejoiced and was glad.

= (Dan 5:7, KJV) =

The king cried aloud to bring in the astrologers, the chaldeans and the soothsayers, and the king spake and said to the wise men of babylon, whosoever shall read this writing, and shew me the interpretation thereof, shall be clothed with scarlet and shall have a chain of gold around his neck, and shall be the third ruler in the whole Kingdom .

= (Acts 12:21, KJV) =

And upon a set day, Herod, arrayed in a royal apparel sat up on the throne, and made an oration unto them.

Mordecai and Daniel are two among God's people who served as royal officials in their various locations at their own different times. From the royal services of these church members we are to be rational about the traditional royal attires worn by God faithful. If wearing traditional royal attires both as a royal traditional servant or aristocrat are all condemned by God , it then means that all of God's people who at any time wear the traditional attires for royal services or aristocrats clothing and other accessories: do commit sin by wearing of traditional royal attires. But putting discretion through a light of farther clarity between some of the God justified and the God condemned traditional royal attires, we should therefore endeavour to remain loyal to God's laws of righteousness by moderate dressing . And we should realise that God will not always condemn most of traditional royal dressings so long as the dressings are not intended to lure the people into sinning. Furthermore; Whether as servants or family members in the traditional royal groups, the focus of the God's people should remain absolute humility to God both through outward and moral decency of dressing: knowing that it is a means of moderating dressing, contentment and righteousness to God.

Chapter 16

MODERATING SPENDING.

DEFINITION = 1 = The act of using up resources wisely.

2 = Being appropriate with giving out money and all other potentials in one's possession.

INTRODUCTION

With no exception from all the previous chapters of the book, we are to be diligent with whatever we do, so we should not settle at mediocre performance or we over do to transgress, causing ourselves and others some harms by either of the mediocrity or trespasses. Incompetence is a weakness and exaggeration is an abuse, so we are to really be moderate in everything of life, so to be contented and not to be frustrated and depressed.

This part of the lesson is to disclose some principles of being moderate and contented with our spending lifestyle. There are so gross number of resources God has given to us humans, though only the minority of us can recognise all of them as resources while the majority are unable to make use of the majority of the resources for anything because they don't understand their values. But those who recognise the value of all the resources and make good use of them are serving God, serving humanity and themselves inclusive, And they're making great fortunes out of them. There also those who recognise most of the potentials and their values, employing them in their ventures but either their stinginess or extravagance makes them to misspend the resources together with the fortunes they make from them. You are to get some great insight on how to moderate your spending of tangible and intangible resources and to build your contentment for securing your peace, happiness and joy on the basis of your wise spending. To learn extensively about wise spending you have to read my book titled = **LIVING A GENEROUS LIFE (From points of reality).**

---

i = DILIGENT PLANNING = (Prov 21:5 NKJV).

The plans of the diligent lead surely to plenty, But those of everyone who is hasty, surely to poverty.

Planning is the first step to actualising visions, dreams or goals. But bad planning is a sabotage to good goals. I know there are good and there are bad goals but I'm focusing on moderation and contentment. So the analysis is about good goals with good planning to realising them. Those who fail to plan alongside their goal in most cases encounter failure due to their rash moves to materialising their goals. Most people are yet to know that direction is more important than speed. For that those who are ignorant of this truth run speedily to actualising their visions but running off targets and running in the wrong directions and to the wrong destinations. Planning is the direction, wrong planning is a wrong direction, good planning is the right direction while the failure to plan is the plan to fail. Diligent plans are good pressures that can be spent into good visions to run them successfully and overcome failure. When this is achieved contentment of accomplishments becomes the evidence.

ii = APPLYING PREVEVENTIVE WISDOM = (Prov 22:3 NKJV).

A prudent man foresees evil and hides himself, But the simple pass on and are punished

= (Prov 27:12 NKJV) =

A prudent man foresees evil and hides himself; The simple pass on and are punished.

Wisdom is one of the greatest treasures that should be spent with a strict caution. The ability to prevent some problems and dangers from manifesting against the preventive people is a segment of wisdom. There are people who play the fool by either not caring about the consequences of any of their predetermined actions or by intentionally ignoring the consequences and endanger themselves into the odd consequences. So applying the wisdom for prevention is the key to moderating our moves into events and, relationships and actions, and to dodge the detected problems then save our peace and stay contented.

iii = APPLYING CREATIVE WISDOM = (Prov 24:3-4 NKJV).

[3] Through wisdom a house is built, And by understanding it is established; [4] By knowledge the rooms are filled With all precious and pleasant riches.

God created the universe with wisdom, and this earth is our own visible evidence of the creation, Moreover we humans are the super product of the same creation. God created us in the replication of his own potentials, so the wisdom for creativity is one of our divine inherent potentials. And for us to live in contentment about fabrication and consumption we must apply our creativity. Creativity and the wisdom powering it makes unquantifiable differences between developed nations, developing nations and non developing nations around the world. Some individual persons are thriving just because they're creative in one or more areas of adventures while some are stagnant and backward just because they're non creative. There are things we should depend on others and God to do for us and there are some things we must do for ourselves, and without creative wisdom we can never do what we must do for ourselves and will never be contented in life just for not doing those things. Everyone as I said earlier has the potential for innovation but the difference is either employing it to achieving good purposes, employing it to achieving bad purposes or keeping it stagnant to stay unproductive in the area of the potential and be dissatisfied in it. Accomplishing good purposes by being wisely creative gives some certain happiness, contentment and joy.

*iv = **GIVING WISE MENTORING** = (Prov 24:6 NKJV).*

***For by wise counsel you will wage your own war, And in a
multitude of counselors there is safety.***

Giving of wise advises is one of the ways to moderate the
spending of the word of the mouth. Bad advising, the boths
of true and false witnessing, fair judgement and unfair
judgement, good commendation and flattery, blessing and
cursing, are some of the ways to spend the words of the mouth
altogether. But using advising as a case example we are to
refrain from offering bad advises to people because with it
we cause discontentment to those we advise and the same
discontentment from the bad result of the bad advises returns
to us the advisers in addition to the restless conscience we
already have for giving the advises even before they backfire.
But when we give the right advises we have settled conscience
whether the beneficiaries take and apply the advises or not.
More than that, the beneficiaries will be contented if they invest
the advises and get the necessary results, and their failure to
be contented therein is an expression of their ungratefulness.
We also fill more contented when people testify that our good
advises help them to succeed in some ways. God is contented
when we humans apply his advises in our life and he's more
contented when we live victoriously through our application
of his advises.

*v = **GIVING HOSPITABLE ATTENTION** = (Prov, 27:23, 26-27 NKJV).*

***[23] Be diligent to know the state of your flocks, And attend
to your herds; [26] The lambs will provide your clothing, And
the goats the price of a field; [27] You shall have enough***

goats' milk for your food, For the food of your household,
And the nourishment of your maidservants.

Attention is a great potential that must be acknowledged in every area of life. Some people abuse attention because they don't know the value. An example is some people having the attitude of disrespecting those who use their time, energy and perhaps good words in attendance of some meetings or whatever with any regard to their attendance. Some people who are disregarded and disrespected when they give attendance and attention to some people secretly or openly withdraw their attendance and attention rather than quarrelling over it. There are some people who prefer to be quarrelling with those who never regard them and their attention for whatever reason. However: it's important we know the value of attention and to know how to spend it wisely. This is to further explain that, we should protect our happiness, peace and joy by restricting and withdrawing our attention from those who not just disregard it for sometimes but from those who choose to never regard it. Moreover we are to give attention to people with genuine intentions, and attending to them with hospitality is the key factor in this case.

vi = PAYING BUSINESS ATTENTION = (Prov 27:23,26-27, NKJV).

[23] Be diligent to know the state of your flocks, And attend to your herds; [26] The lambs will provide your clothing, And the goats the price of a field; [27] You shall have enough goats' milk for your food, For the food of your household, And the nourishment of your maidservants.

In whichever means of income we have engaged in there is the obligatory attention we should be giving to it, so we can constantly know the state of affairs of the income revenues, to maintain them when necessary and to ensure the way we keep them is intact and to make sure we harness every advantage they can produce. By doing this, we can be happy and contented with the benefits from those businesses. Some people suffer disappointment and frustration in businesses not because they don't understand the investment and trading secrets of the businesses but just because they fail to recognise the role of consistent attendance to know how their businesses are going, whether forward, backward or stagnant. And before they should realise some damages in the businesses it becomes late for them to recover their due dividends of the ventures.

*vii = **INVESTING YOUR MONEY** = (1st Cor 16:2 NKJV).*

On the first day of the week let each one of you lay something aside, storing up as he may prosper, that there be no collections when I come.

Money is a powerful servant tool that contributes to the greatness of those who make it their servant. Because as I speak, there are people who don't know yet that their money should be their servant, so they keep their money stagnant, spend it lavishly or they serve their own money by permitting money to control them or being afraid to get much more because they believe they can't handle it. Investment is aimed at attracting profits so investing the money is a tantamount to attracting more money. A stagnant money is an unproductive money, a wasted money is a waste to the waster but a benefit to the patronised. Wrongly invested money is a wasted money by misfortune.

The three people Jesus gave one, two and five talents to each of the three for investment are practical examples of how different peoples regard money. The first person among the three was given five talents and he invested it to double it, the second receiving two talents did the same, but the third kept his own stagnant by burying it, all of them doing this until the time of their accounting to the master Jesus Christ. The wisely investing two servants of Jesus were contented with Jesus commendation for their good job, while the third was contented for not investing but blaming Jesus for having given him the talent. However the third person was eventually discontented with Jesus condemnation to his idleness and unproductivity even while the servant tool for production was in his possession.

ix = ADAPTING TO TIME DIFFERENCES = (Eccl 3:1-8 NKJV).

[1] To everything there is a season, A time for every purpose under heaven: [2] A time to be born, And a time to die; A time to plant, And a time to pluck what is planted; [3] A time to kill, And a time to heal; A time to break down, And a time to build up; [4] A time to weep, And a time to laugh; A time to mourn, And a time to dance; [5] A time to cast away stones, And a time to gather stones; A time to embrace, And a time to refrain from embracing; [6] A time to gain, And a time to lose; A time to keep, And a time to throw away; [7] A time to tear, And a time to sew; A time to keep silence, And a time to speak; [8] A time to love, And a time to hate; A time of war, And a time of peace.

Some people are living in frustration and hopelessness just because they fail to observe and live by the trending necessities of the time. Many of the recent contemporaries are living in the past in as much as they're not yet in tune with the current products, happenings, informations and good patterns. There are positivities and negativities in every contemporary, so some people of each of the contemporaries can suffer setbacks if they're tuned to the negativities. But those who fix themselves into the current positivities of each time never fail and suffer setbacks. Most people fail in their life just because they do the right thing at the wrong times. So people may have the right intention, right knowledge and right actions and still fail because they don't perform according to time propriety. For us to be truly wise, prosperous and successful we have to learn and adapt to knowing what to do and what not to do at each times of the day, of the week, of the month, of the year, of the decade and of the century. The prosperity and success for doing this include living in satisfaction which is being contented.

x = SPENDING YOUR SEX LIFE = (Prov 5:18-20 NKJV).

[18] Let your fountain be blessed, And rejoice with the wife of your youth. [19] As a loving deer and a graceful doe, Let her breasts satisfy you at all times; And always be enraptured with her love. [20] For why should you, my son, be enraptured by an immoral woman, And be embraced in the arms of a seductress?

= (Prov 31:2-3 NKJV) =

[2] What, my son? And what, son of my womb? And what, son of my vows? [3] Do not give your strength to women, Nor your ways to that which destroys kings.

No other person should have sex with you except your wife or your husband. The past sex most of us had when we were or even as some of us are still unmarried and the past sex married men and married women had outside of their marriage is all sin. God originally and forever institutes sex for marriage life between each husband and only one wife, but rebellion to the will of God make selfish humans to invent sex perversions of all kinds. Sex does not sustain relationships and even monogamous marriage where good characters and self discipline are lacking. Even where good characters are available in polygamy lack of self discipline which resulted in the marriage of one man with two or more wives becomes the foundation of troubles which erupt from such a marriage. There are lots of troubles sex bring to people involved in premarital or extramarital sex, because God is not in support of such sex life and never blesses them and the participants. But contentment in sex life is an inheritance to any monogamous couple whose marriage is governed by God and them loving each other with godly love.

xi = SPENDING YOUR DOMINION AUTHORITY =
   (Prov 31:2-3 NKJV).

[2] What, my son? And what, son of my womb? And what, son of my vows? [3] Do not give your strength to women, Nor your ways to that which destroys kings.

Kings are leaders with dominion authority over certain territories and over the people of the communities which they rule. God's people are kings and priests who should be reigning in Righteousness with dominion authority in this world. This is the reason God created man and gave them the dominion authority over other creatures in the first place, but the flaws of Adam and his wife Eve made them lose it to the serpentine Lucifer whose voice they bowed to and forsook God's own voice for them. Samson lost his dominion power to Delilah and his down fall began. King Ahab lost his dominion authority to his idolatrous wife Jezebel then began national idolatry in Israel. King Solomon lost his dominion authority to his seven hundred idolatrous wives who led him into idolatry and used him to extend the idolatry nationwide in Israel. There are many histories of those who mismanaged their dominion authority and of those who utilised it. Jesus Christ came to this earth to win the dominion authority back from satan and to the redeemed humanity, so some of us are making good use of it while some have lost it again back to satan. Satan is subject to few Christians and some few others but he's in control of the majority of the Christians and others who have lost their dominion power to him absolutely. Nobody can live a truly satisfied life after he had lost that dominion authority, but the few who still retain theirs use it as a key potent to command and control their own situations excelling over them and glorifying God for that.

*xii = **SEEKING PLEASURE AND COMFORT** = (Prov 24:3-4, NKJV).*

[3] Through wisdom a house is built, And by understanding it is established; [4] By knowledge the rooms are filled With all precious and pleasant riches.

= (Isaiah 5:22 NKJV) =

Woe to men mighty at drinking wine, Woe to men valiant for mixing intoxicating drink.

= (Proverbs 31:4-7 NKJV) =

[4] It is not for kings, O Lemuel, It is not for kings to drink wine, Nor for princes intoxicating drink; [5] Lest they drink

and forget the law, And pervert the justice of all the afflicted. [6] Give strong drink to him who is perishing, And wine to those who are bitter of heart. [7] Let him drink and forget his poverty, And remember his misery no more.

The concept of business before pleasure is very essential in all we do in life, even God implemented the same wisdom in life by programming it that eternal life and eternal pleasure and comfort should be the upmost priority of humanity. Some people end their life in dissatisfaction because they prefer early and temporary pleasures and comfort to enjoy and that costing them their time, energy and other resources which they spend to meet that pleasure and comfort. At times the pleasure and comfort may not be in some sinful ways but it makes them to venture far more minimal and settle in mediocrity then never strive for excellence. This is evident in some genuine Christians who make it to heaven and to discover they are just common citizens who have no houses of their own and are not employed in any of heavenly functions, just because they only invested their hearts, body spirit and soul into heaven but never invested their resources and services.

There are other kinds of Christians who like most of the non Christians who prefer pleasures and comforts of sin, to those of eternal comfort through consistent righteous living. So as such don't invest anything in heaven and they have no place in it, so they spend all of their own pleasure and comfort here on earth and eternal suffering in the hell fire is their end. Regarding financial life there are people who suffer in the old age when they're unable to work actively anymore just because they lavished their money and some other values to have pleasure and comfort in their youthful ages. But there are people who live a glorious life in their old ages with some investments they made during their youthful ages.

The cases of the two sets of people are no different from ours: we should make the right choice and right decision to prepare our avenues of pleasure and comfort for our old age and to begin implementing them from now. We are also to prepare more especially for our eternal pleasure and comfort in God's kingdom.

OTHER BOOKS BY EVANGELIST INYIMA KALU.

1 = LUSTS AND THEIR PROBLEMS. (From points of reality).

3 = POLYGAMY AND ITS PROBLEMS. (From points of reality).

3 = THE OLIVETH PROPHECY = Matthew 24. (From points of reality).

EPILOGUE

All of God's laws are aimed at discipline prompted by moderation and the utmost result is contentment, which is being satisfied with what God provides and to live within them. God has all it takes for all of us humans to live in satisfaction but only the minute really live in satisfaction due to the inability of the vast majority to live within the boundaries of God's rules for everything.

Starting with Adam and Eve in the garden of Eden God made everything they needed available and for them to enjoy them for eternity but their rebellion to him sabotaged the whole show, turning their failure and suffering consequences a transgenerational to the entire mankind, due to a transgenerational continuation of humans rebellion to God.

> *Rom 3:23 NKJV = for all have sinned and fall short of the glory of God,*

There had been some traces of sin in the life of each person before the coming of Jesus Christ for universal redemption of the sinful humans. This further explains that the sin in the life of each person could never allow the full manifestation of God's glorious purpose in the life of each of them. However: the coming of Jesus then was to pay for the sin of man, to eradicate the sin from the life of man and to restore the intended glory of God for all round of satisfaction in the life of the man.

Rom = 6:23 NKJV = For the wages of sin is death, but the gift of God is eternal life in Christ Jesus our Lord.

Believing in the redemption work of Jesus Christ, making him the lord of life by living to please him in everything is the only way to getting back the lost glory and to enjoy contentment in all respect for eternity. The born again Christians who are also financially and health-wise comfortable are the only set of people that truly live in universal contentment, because others may be financially and health-wise comfortable as well or even more than the born again Christians, yet they never can live in contentment because they lack the absolutely wellbeing of the spirit and soul.

3rd John 1:2-4 NKJV = [2] Beloved, I pray that you may prosper in all things and be in health, just as your soul prospers. [3] For I rejoiced greatly when brethren came and testified of the truth that is in you, just as you walk in the truth. [4] I have no greater joy than to hear that my children walk in truth.

Only the born again Christians can afford to live by the truth which is the undiluted word of God personified and characterised by Jesus Christ. Truth is incomplete in any life without Jesus Christ, so all of the non Christians live either by half truth of a total lie. The majority of the Christians are not born again however. So it's only the fewest among the church attendees are genuinely regenerated in soul, spirit, body and character. Any non born again can become one just from now and is allowed to overtake the already born again.

THE AUTHOR

Inyima Kalu: is an anointed teacher of God's Word, who had undergone some theological mentoring through which he became an excellent learner of the truth about God, His words, and will, with accurate understanding, also being helped by his real Christian upbringing from childhood, And by the grace of God, he attended Christian discipleship study at the Redeemed Christian Church of God, Valencia, Spain/(2010). He is thoroughly mentored on almost all aspects of doctrines at (Christ the King Ministry), Valencia, Spain [2011-2019]. From 2019, he became a Bible teacher in Assemblies of God Church (Beautiful Gate) Parish, Valencia, Spain. Moreover, Inyima Kalu is regular with Bible research for regular discoveries of godly realities and truths. He is an evangelist in the five hold ministries.

Ephesians 4:11, Amplified Classic =

And His gifts were [varied; He Himself appointed and gave men to us] some to be apostles (special messengers), some prophets (inspired preachers and expounders), some evangelists (preachers of the Gospel, traveling missionaries), some pastors (shepherds of His flock) and teachers.

Combining his evangelical oration, perspective(s), exploration of the revelations from God's Word, and his teaching potential, he began to develop and document some lessons of which this book is a part. Though no human church leader had ordained Inyima Kalu: he has God's spiritual empowerment and inspiration and grace to divide God's Word accurately from God's own perspectives, regarding all aspects of life and adventures. As God progresses Evangelist, Inyima Kalu, his ministry has advanced, and he has become an evangelical writer. Beyond discovery and teaching, Inyima believes in living by good example according to God's will and purpose. More so, he is an online teacher and runs the (Evangelist Inyima Kalu) YouTube and Facebook and Instagram.

Evangelist Inyima Kalu hails from [Ohafia in Abia State, Nigeria]. He was born into a parish of a Pentecostal Church – [Christ Holy Church](Nation Builders) in his home town, Ebem Ohafia, were he was brought up from his childhood.

While undergoing doctrinal tutelage in Christ the King Ministry, Valencia, Spain, he became an acting pastor from 2014-2019. He was joined to the church board of the said Assemblies of God Church where he is currently a parishioner. He has being a Pentecostal Christian all through his life.

He is resident in Valencia, Spain.